Privacy and Libel Law:
The Clash with Press Freedom

Privacy and Libel Law: The Clash with Press Freedom

Paul Tweed
Senior Partner, Johnsons Solicitors

Bloomsbury Professional

Bloomsbury Professional Ltd, Maxwelton House, 41–43 Boltro Road, Haywards Heath, West Sussex, RH16 1BJ

© Paul Tweed 2012

Bloomsbury Professional Ltd is an imprint of Bloomsbury Publishing plc

A CIP Catalogue record for this book is available from the British Library.

ISBN 978 1 84766 902 5

Typeset by Phoenix Photosetting Ltd, Chatham, Kent
Printed and bound in Great Britain by Martins the Printers, Berwick-upon-Tweed, Northumberland

Preface

Even my four decades of a love-hate relationship with the press provided no forewarning as to the intense and divisive dramas that would emanate from the phone hacking scandal, not to mention the "super injunction" and "libel tourism" controversies. The newspaper headlines continue to be dominated with sensational stories of Premier League footballers attempting to keep their illicit affairs under wraps, international personalities seeking to protect their reputations and ever more valuable brands, the MPs expenses scandal and all sorts of shenanigans involving those in public life, with the tabloids and broadsheets vying to outsmart each other in an increasingly competitive market.

In many respects, these sensational developments have been a lawyer's dream and have resulted in me having the privilege of addressing a House of Commons Joint Committee on Defamation and several Ministry of Justice Panels set up to review UK libel law. I have also had the opportunity of putting forward arguments in support of our privacy and libel laws by way of presentations to a number of Bar Associations in the US. In attempting to highlight the difficulties facing the ordinary man and his lack of access to justice never mind freedom of speech, I have generally received a very positive response in California, in contrast to somewhat overt hostility in New York. Whether this reflects the more liberal thinking on the east coast of the United States, or Manhattan's closer proximity to the UK, I am not sure, but suffice to say I do not see any prospect of a strengthening of US libel laws any time soon!

I have however nothing but admiration for the incredibly effective lobbying campaign organised by the US publishing associations and other interested parties, which resulted in President Obama signing off on the Speech Act in what must have been record time, notwithstanding the other distractions the Government and country had been facing in terms of the serious economic crisis.

In this book I have endeavoured to let the facts speak for themselves, leaving the readership to participate like a jury in deciding on the merits of the various scenarios. Indeed, it is perhaps ironic that the public will soon be deprived of any judgemental role in defamation actions, if the current recommendations are ultimately enacted into law, and the right to a jury trial effectively abolished in all but the most exceptional cases.

While I have endeavoured to incorporate the recent developments and evidence to the likes of the Leveson Inquiry in my view, this entire area of law remains very much a moving feast. However, one thing is certain, and that is the need for reform of the current system of press regulation and at least an element of clarification of the laws relating to privacy and defamation.

Regardless of where you stand in the increasingly emotive battle between freedom of expression and the right to privacy and reputation, I hope that the approach I have taken in the following chapters will provide a useful insight and some food for thought when you are next reading your morning newspaper.

I for one hope this will remain a treasured national pastime for many years to come, notwithstanding the increasing threat to the traditional media from online publications. However, I firmly believe that the interests of the press on both sides of the Atlantic are best served, and indeed protected, by the maintenance of high standards in terms of quality journalism and fair and accurate reporting. The question therefore is whether this can best be achieved by robust statutory or other regulation.

PAUL TWEED
January 2012

Acknowledgments

Special thanks to three of Johnsons' lawyers, Kathy Mathews, Laura Cunningham and James Ead for their invaluable contributions to the book. I am also grateful to Fintan Drury, who clearly has retained his skills as a former journalist in assisting with the edit along with my daughter Shannon Tweed, whose editing work bodes well for her future career. I could not have completed the book without the guidance and suggestions from my wife and fellow lawyer Selena, and David Craig, one of my loyal partners in Johnsons.

I also must pay tribute to my long suffering PAs Betty Currie and Diane Worthington, who have had to cope with not only consistent deadlines but also my impatience and the various other day to day distractions that are part and parcel of a lawyer's working life.

Finally, I must thank Paul Feldstein for introducing me to Andy Hill, the Head of Legal Publishing at Bloomsbury, whose guidance and advice has been invaluable in the long haul to reach publication.

Contents

Table of Cases

Table of Cases

Introduction

"The worst thing that can happen to a man is to lose his money, the next worst his health, the next worst his reputation"

(Samuel Butler)

Notwithstanding a decade of almost continuous decline in the number of defamation Actions coming before the UK Courts, we have somewhat inexplicably seen a dramatic increase in the attention given by the press to an area of law that many people had dismissed as the preserve of the rich and famous. However, prompted by a smattering of claims initiated by a relatively small band of Hollywood celebrities, the press decided to embark on what could be regarded as one of the most disproportionate and unnecessary campaigns for law reform in recent memory.

The original focus had been what has come to be known as *"Libel Tourism"* or *"Forum Shopping"* by wealthy American stars and Russian oligarchs, who were perceived to be taking advantage of Britain's more stringent libel laws in order to protect, not just their reputations, but, often just as importantly, their business empires.

Powerful media interests, perceiving a potentially serious threat to their own financial strength, lost no time in clamouring for an urgent change in the law to prevent what they regarded as an outrageous and inappropriate practice.

However, as what were often one-sided commentaries began to gain momentum, the clamour for reform was extended to encompass a further demand for wholesale changes in order to bring the UK legislation in line with the First Amendment and other rights prevailing in the United States.

The general public could be forgiven for thinking that our libel laws constitute an obvious and incontestable flaw in the UK legal system and as such have been bringing the whole country into contempt and turning the Courts into a laughing stock. The press of course have, and will likely always have, full control of the presentation of the arguments and, aided and abetted by their colleagues in the US, did not take too long to persuade the political establishment that reform was necessary. The last Labour Government set the ball rolling by setting up various Committees, to at least give the appearance that the situation was being addressed, with the politicians on both sides of the House conscious at all times of the need to ensure that the press were placated, particularly with a General Election in the offing.

Unfortunately for Labour, their actions were insufficient to prevent their total humiliation at the ballot box but, almost immediately on the formation of a new government, the Conservative/Lib Dem Coalition assumed Labour's policy position and initiated a review of the libel laws. After taking office, Deputy Prime Minister Nick Clegg, in a apparent attempt to curry favour with the media establishment, began condemning our libel laws to anyone who would listen and proclaiming that they *"make a mockery of British justice"*[1]. It appeared that the media and political establishments were ad idem on the need for reform of our libel laws.

Then to paraphrase Harold MacMillan, "events" occurred that were to undermine on the surface at least, the depth of that relationship when in the summer of 2011 the breadth and depth of the phone hacking scandal first emerged. Even those newspapers who had previously been robust and uncompromising in their criticism of not only the law of libel but also the increasingly debated rights to privacy and confidentiality, suddenly had to get off their campaigning horse and acknowledge what was rapidly becoming one of the greatest scandals of the 21st Century. Right up until July, 2011, the mainstream press and their online counterparts had been concentrating on their sometimes hysterical condemnation of the super-injunctions and what they perceived to be a totally unacceptable threat to their right to freedom of expression.

Somewhat surprisingly, it was only when the phone hacking scandal touched upon the lives of ordinary people and victims of crime such as Milly Dowler, that the press realised that they had to proceed with considerable caution in their reporting of an issue that had touched the public conscience in a way that a sex scandal involving a professional footballer never could. However, what is perhaps just as surprising is that the Information Commissioner's Reports into "Operation Motorman" published some five years earlier, detailing extensive breaches of personal privacy and confidentiality, barely received a mention in the press.

This somewhat questionable scenario serves to highlight both the power of the press and what could be regarded as a total disregard for the rights of the ordinary man on the street whose interests have been totally ignored during what has been one of the most high profile issues debated in modern times.

At this point, you may be forgiven for thinking that I am just as guilty of the same unbalanced approach of which I am criticising the press, but in this book I will be seeking to put all the facts on the table and will leave the reader to decide, in the same manner as any jury, on the evidence. I would however submit that in acting for both Claimants and Defendant publishers I have had the experience of understanding the sentiments on both sides, and operating from offices in London, Dublin and Belfast has given me the benefit of assessing the laws relating to privacy and defamation in three separate jurisdictions, with their subtle distinctions.

And by way of additional special pleading, I should also point out that the largest single group of Claimant clients for whom I act is made up of journalists, with the second largest group comprising of lawyers. I would suggest the fact that these

---

1   Speech to the Royal Society, 18 January 2010 (see: http://news.bbc.co.uk/1/hi/uk_politics/8466297. stm)

two groups will be very familiar with media law and practice provides an indication that they know when a wrong has been committed and when they should be entitled to redress.

I should also point out that I have generally enjoyed a good relationship with individual editors, journalists and in-house lawyers, and indeed, it may come as some surprise that I regard several of the tabloid editors to be among some of the most honourable opponents I have come across in more than 30 years as a media lawyer.

And so who or what is behind the so called clash with press freedom? Although it was Britain who provided America with the basis for their defamation laws, or what is left of them, we have to cross the Atlantic in order to understand not only the current differences in the law, but also the basis for the recent clamour for reform.

Chapter 1

Background to the controversy – differences in attitudes towards "freedom of speech" in the US and UK

"There are only two occasions when Americans respect privacy, especially in Presidents. Those are prayer and fishing".

(Herbert Hoover)

On 10 August, 2010, President Obama signed a somewhat draconian piece of legislation into the US statute books after months of intense pressure from professional PR specialists, publishers associations and various political and other lobbyists. The SPEECH Act[1] was not only uncompromising, but some would also say totally unnecessary, given that its objective, the prevention of enforcement of foreign libel judgments in the US Courts, was already virtually impossible in that country. The title of the Act was in itself an acronym for *"Securing the Protection of our Enduring and Established Constitutional Heritage"*, but its purpose was to act as a high profile deterrent to any American citizen having the temerity to consider suing a US publisher abroad.

The case that set in motion what was an extremely effective campaign, was a fairly low key libel Action brought in the High Court in London by a Saudi Arabian entrepreneur, Sheikh Bin Mahfouz, against New York based author, Dr Rachel Ehrenfeld[2] over defamatory allegations contained in her controversial book, *"Funding Evil. How Terrorism is Financed and How To Stop It"*. The book was first published in the United States in August, 2003, less than two years following the September 11 suicide terrorist attacks on the Twin Towers of the World Trade Centre and the the Pentagon.

The author, Dr Ehrenfeld, had held herself out as *"the world's foremost authority on narcoterrorism... and a sought after commentator and consultant on the problems of international terrorism."* The subject matter of the book unsurprisingly focused on the financing of international terrorism. Ehrenfeld had identified Mahfouz and his

1   HR 2765
2   [2005] EWHC 1156 (QB)

family as being one of the main sponsors of Al Qaeda and other terror organisations, and had alleged that Mahfouz provided financial assistance to the illegal groups by various means including channelling funds to Saudi based charities which, in 1999, were alleged fronts for Al Qaeda pre-9/11. Libel actions were brought in both the US and the UK, the latter after it became known that 23 copies of the book had been purchased in the UK through online retailers. The UK action was also based on the open publication of the first chapter of the book on the ABC TV channel's news website.

Ehrenfeld initially did respond to the claim through her attorneys before proceedings were commenced in the UK, indicating that she would be in a position to prove the validity of the allegations. However, ultimately she decided not to formally come on record in the Action, thereby totally undermining her ability to substantiate the extremely serious allegations of terrorist involvement levelled at Mr Mahfouz. Accordingly, judgment was entered against Ehrenfeld in default of her failing to file a Defence. In his judgment for summary disposal of the case, ruling in favour of Mahfouz, Mr Justice Eady made a declaration of falsity against the publication; having heard evidence prepared by the lawyers acting for Mahfouz that he considered would have entirely justified the Sheik's vindication. The court awarded a substantial six figure sum in damages, together with legal costs against Ehrenfeld. What is interesting and of no little significance is the fact that, despite this ruling, no attempt was made by the Claimant to enforce the damages and costs award against Ms Ehrenfeld in the US. This point was conveniently overlooked by many of those who began clamouring for reform in the aftermath of the decision. Certainly, the frenetic lobbying for legislation to prevent the enforcement of UK libel judgments in the US, which was prompted by the Ehrenfeld action, appears to have been somewhat misguided, and indeed unnecessary, given that it would have been virtually impossible to persuade a US Court to enforce such a judgment even before the introduction of the divisive SPEECH Act.

Perhaps it was also notable that in the course of his judgment there was already a palpable tension, where Eady J referred to numerous statements that Ehrenfeld had allegedly made stateside, which suggested that she had deliberately chosen not to defend the case on the basis that, as well as apparently being financially restricted, she considered that it was impossible to defend a case in the jurisdiction due to the UK's "pro-Plaintiff" libel laws. Eady J had sternly rebutted this proposition in his dicta:

> "The purpose of this exercise [Ehrenfeld's remonstration] is fairly obvious, namely to give the impression that any judgement of the English court is of little significance and does nothing to establish that the allegations are false. That is why it is so important, as the claimants appreciate, to go through such allegations as have been made against them in the past, on behalf of these defendants in order to demonstrate their lack of merit. That is why this judgement has gone to such length. It is not purely a formal process and the declaration of falsity which I propose to grant shortly is not an empty gesture."[3]

3   Ibid, para 72 per Eady J

In a sense, these words of Mr Justice Eady lie somewhere near the core of the rationale that has sustained the UK's libel laws over the centuries – to establish that any damaging allegations which may be published and which are not supported by some form of credible research or evidence, are false. Although the case itself attracted little attention at the time, primarily due to Dr Ehrenfeld's decision not to appear in Court to justify her allegations, the author's subsequent campaign and efforts to block the enforcement of the judgment against her in the US gave rise to what was probably the most effective lobbying and media campaign since that orchestrated by the tobacco industry several decades ago.

While we in the UK, and Northern Ireland in particular, have been accustomed to Defendants refusing to recognise the Court on political grounds, this approach had normally been confined to accused members of the Provisional IRA, who had successfully adopted this strategy during the three decades of their campaign. Accordingly, it was somewhat ironic that the New York legislators would decide to introduce their statute with the title of the Libel Terrorism Protection Act[4]. This legislation, coming about as a direct result of the aforesaid lobbying, was aimed at preventing the enforcement of UK libel judgments in New York State.

One could be forgiven for having to read the title of this Act several times such is the anomaly of its heading, particularly as there no further reference to the word terrorism within the body of the statute. However, it was undoubtedly no coincidence that the spark that had ignited this firestorm of reform was a libel case related to the contents of a book about America's then newest spectres, Global Terrorism and Al Qaeda.

Congressman Peter King, a New York (Long Island) Republican stated on the floor of the House of Representatives that[5]:

> *"Libel tourism threatens not only Americans' first amendment freedom of speech but also their ability to inform the general public about existential threats, namely the identity of terrorists and their financial supporters. In many of these cases, journalists are trying to write on topics of national and homeland security."*

And...

> *"I receive regular classified briefings on dangerous plots to attack the United States, so I know just how grave these threats are. We cannot allow foreigners the ability to muzzle Americans for speaking the truth about these dangers,"*

Another member of this committee, Congressman Steve Cohen, who introduced the Bill for the SPEECH Act to the House of Representatives,[6] was also quoted by the *Guardian* newspaper:

---

4   Libel Terrorism Protection Act S 6687/A 9652
5   http://judiciary.house.gov/hearings/printers/111th/111-4_47316.PDF
6   HR 2765

"England has become the favourite destination of libel tourists from around the world, especially wealthy tourists from countries whose own laws are downright hostile to free speech"[7]

King quoted himself on his Congressional website when introducing the proposed 2009 Bill as follows:

"Our journalists provide us with insight on issues that affect all Americans, such as war and terrorism. We cannot allow their voices to be silenced by those who prefer to keep secret the inner details of these issues. American authors and journalists should be able to practice their First Amendment right without the fear of a lawsuit."[8]

In an article penned by King for the Rupert Murdoch owned *New York Post* dated 6 October 2008 he stated in a similar vein:

"Nothing in my Bill would limit the rights of foreign litigants who bring good faith defamation actions … it does, however, try to discourage those foreign suits that aim to intimidate, threaten and restrict the freedom of speech of Americans."[9]

It was abundantly clear that, notwithstanding the declaration of falsity and Mahfouz's subsequent success against Ehrenfeld in the state Court in New York based on that declaration, no consideration was to be given to the prospect that Ehrenfeld's allegations had not been substantiated. The New York State *Libel Terrorism Protection Act* was ultimately sponsored by Assemblyman Rory Lancman (D-Queens) and Senator Dean Skelos (R-LI), both of the New York State Legislature, and was signed into law by Governor Patterson on 29 April 2009. The Act prevented the enforcement of foreign libel judgments against citizens of the United States in the State of New York in absolute terms. Congressman King went on to introduce the first Bill that would attempt to implement this law on a national scale, the Free Speech Protection Act of 2008.[10] He was later co-sponsor for a further Bill, *"to amend... the United States Code, to prohibit recognition and enforcement of foreign defamation judgments"*[11], also in 2008, which preceded a number of Bills culminating in the passing of the SPEECH Act of 2010. The Bill that proceeded before the Senate[12] was sponsored by Senator Patrick Leahy (Vermont). Leahy, having been appointed to his chair in the Senate 1975, also had contemporary vitriol for anything that would impinge on the American's right to free speech.

Bills were passed unanimously in both the House of Representatives and the Senate illustrating the depth of fervour for the prevalence of the First Amendment free

---

7   "US Congress presses Britain to amend 'harmful' libel law", 23 February 2009: http://www.guardian. co.uk/uk/2009/feb/23/us-congress-britain-libel-law)
8   http://www.house.gov/apps/list/press/ny03_king/PR030509.html
9   http://www.nypost.com
10   HR 5184
11   HR 6146
12   Section 3518

speech over the English common law, that had historically underpinned America's own libel laws.

It is important to acknowledge Dr Ehrenfeld's determination and focus in striving to protect those First Amendment rights that have been so firmly embedded in the American psyche. Indeed, it is difficult to fault the basic thinking of those early pioneers behind the drafting of the US Constitution, against the background of a young nation striving to find its identity while seeking to protect and encourage such a diverse diaspora of people who had come to the country in search of a better life. Of even more significance was the fact that many of these new patriots had fled to America to escape persecution at home, where the right to speak your mind and express an opinion was simply not an option for those holding a minority ethnic or religious viewpoint in their own country. Accordingly, "freedom of speech" was very much at the top of the agenda in drafting the Constitution, and remains so to this day. This is in itself a noble principle but the problem, however, is that those early draftsmen could not possibly have foreseen the rapid rise of international reputations crossing not just borders but huge continents in a matter of seconds, thanks to the development of cross-channel publication and expansion of the world wide web.

Accordingly, just as the American press zealously guards its right to report and allege what it likes, when it likes, it should recognise that its virtually limitless protection under the First Amendment must be open to careful scrutiny, as a result of the aforementioned advances in mass communication and dissemination of information.

The problem is that, immediately a story has been published the damage has been done, and no matter how much is ultimately paid in monetary compensation, the overall damage to the individual's reputation will be irreparable. The same observation applies to an even greater extent to breaches of individual privacy, where once the "privacy horse has bolted" then it is difficult to conceive of a remedy that could possibly put the individual back in the position they had been in before publication.

And thus we have the pivotal struggle between an individual's right to protect their reputation and privacy on the one hand, and the right of the press to report on matters of public interest on the other hand. It is accepted that the media has an important role to play in developed society and it must be free to undertake investigative work in order to expose wrongdoings and corrupt or completely inappropriate behaviour, however, it must do this work in an ethical, balanced and equitable manner.

The following chapters will endeavour to identify the fundamental differences in attitude towards "freedom of speech" on either side of the Atlantic, and to explain how the US, having based its libel laws on our own common law all those years ago, has reached a point where there is now a significant gulf between our respective positions in this important area of law. The US perspective on the damage that can be inflicted on an individual's reputation without remedy is radically different to that held under UK law and the US appears determined to impose its standards of free speech on the rest of the world.

Not only has the SPEECH Act made it incredibly difficult for a US citizen to secure vindication of his reputation against a US publisher abroad, but he also faces the risk of a significant financial penalty if he even attempts to seek redress in the UK Courts. However, it should be borne in mind that this Act only applies to disputes between American citizens being determined in another country. The Act does not, and cannot interfere with the US national's right to sue UK or European publishers in the High Court in London (subject to jurisdictional criteria being satisfied). Nonetheless, the publicity surrounding the introduction of the SPEECH Act is likely to be a deterrent in itself to America, particularly with the extent of the coverage given to this issue by the likes of the *New York Times* and other national broadsheets.

One of the key principles of the SPEECH Act is the complete refusal to recognise foreign defamation judgments. In what some regard as a "knee-jerk" reaction, Section 4102 of the statute declares that a US Court:

> *"shall not recognize or enforce a foreign judgment for defamation whenever the party opposing recognition or enforcement of the judgment claims that the judgment is inconsistent with the first amendment to the Constitution of the United States, unless the domestic court determines that the judgment is consistent with the first amendment ...".*

As John J Walsh, a leading US media lawyer, has argued forcefully to those who will listen, this provision flies in the face of the principle of international comity which requires the mutual recognition by nations of the laws and conventions of other countries on the basis of reciprocity and mutual respect. Indeed the concept of international comity was recognised by the US Supreme Court in 1895 in the case *Hilton v Guyot*[13] in which comity was described as "the recognition which one nation allows within its territory to the legislative, executive, or judicial acts of another nation, having due regard both to international duty and convenience, and to the rights of its own citizens, or of other persons who are under the protection of its laws"[14].

The refusal to recognize libel judgments emanating from outside the US has its origins in the case of *Telnikoff v. Matusevitch*[15] in which a Maryland Court refused to recognize an English libel judgment on the basis that it conflicted with state laws on freedom of the press as well as the First Amendment. The SPEECH Act has followed the judicial reasoning adopted in this case and has codified it in statute. The very essence of comity requires a reasoned analysis of the equivalence of competing and, in some cases, conflicting laws and rights. It would surely then be more appropriate to allow the US Courts the flexibility to exercise their discretion and weigh up the merits of each individual action on a case by case basis.

It is somewhat ironic that the UK is being criticized for allegedly attempting to impose *"pro-claimant"* laws which supposedly *chill* free speech, which is precisely what the US has sought to do in enacting legislation which flatly refuses to recognise

13   159 US 113 (1895)
14   Ibid, para
15   (702 A.2d 230, 251 (Md 1997)

the laws of other nations. In doing so, American publishers of defamatory material are being afforded the blanket protection of US law, regardless of the fact that the offending material is being freely disseminated across the borders of other nations. Many commentators have condemned this legislative move as an attempt to impose US standards, in particular First Amendment concepts of freedom of speech, on other countries. Are we witnessing a new form of legislative imperialism from the United States? The presumption that American protections for free speech are somehow inherently superior to those provided for in Britain and in Europe under the auspices of the ECHR is insulting to say the least. Quite apart from the risk of causing offence to allies and neighbours, there is also a potential risk for the US that other countries may follow suit and refuse to recognize and enforce US laws, a development which would clearly have significant ramifications for foreign relations and the global *"war on terror"*.

This move to frustrate the application of British law possibly calls into question the nature of the 'special relationship' we are reported to enjoy with our American counterparts.

Chapter 2

Development of libel law in the USA

"The will of the people is the only legitimate foundation of any Government, and to protect its free expression should be our first object".

(Thomas Jefferson)

Ironically, prior to 1964, defamation law in the United States was effectively based on English common law, albeit with each individual State introducing variations based on their interpretation of the law. The fundamental principles mirrored those of the English system, namely that the Plaintiff simply had to establish that a Defendant had published material that would harm his reputation, without proof being required as to fault or intention, or the falsity of the content. The burden of proof then lay with the Defendant to attempt to prove that the content of the publication was true, or justified. The basic law pre-dated the American Revolution (1775–1783) and the enforcement of the law after the introduction of the Bill of Rights in 1791 continued without substantial change for some time, notwithstanding the First Amendment right of freedom of speech stating:

"Congress shall make no law... abridging the freedom of speech, or of the press; or the right of the people ... to petition the Government for a redress of grievances."

This is of course one of the cornerstones of the American democratic principles, providing the means by which the people of the United States can challenge authority and maintain the revered objectives that are enshrined in the US Constitution. While historically the First Amendment was the subject of numerous legal challenges relating to the conduct of civil affairs and the laws passed by various States in relation to, inter alia, public order, the US Courts were initially reluctant to address the balance between this fundamental right and the common law relating to libel. This area of law remained relatively unchanged over about 200 years of American legal history. However, the tide of reform did gradually materialise through a number of landmark cases.

Commentators point to the eighteenth century case of *John Peter Zenger* as a forerunner to the more fundamental precedents in respect of the reform of libel law in the United States over the course of the twentieth century, a decision which is also popularly regarded as a landmark case for press freedom. Zenger was the editor of the *New York Weekly Journal*, which campaigned against what it viewed as the intolerable governance of the state of New York by its British Royal Governor, Sir William Cosby. It began publishing anonymous parodies openly criticising Cosby's administration. Zenger was quickly arrested and charged with having published "*a certain false, malicious, seditious, scandalous libel.*" Indeed, he was actually imprisoned for a time in advance of one of America's most famous trials, heard by Mr James DeLancey, Chief Justice of the Province of New York, and Frederick Philipse, Associate Justice on 4 August 1735.

According to Zenger's own record of proceedings, his esteemed attorney, Mr Alexander Hamilton, scythed through the rarefied air of the State Courtroom with the assertion that it was the prosecuting Attorneys who should prove the allegations to be false in order to show that there had been a libel. However, Hamilton went on to offer that[1]:

> "*...we will save [the prosecuting attorney] the trouble of proving a negative, take [it] on ourselves, and prove those very papers that are called libels to be true.*"

The Chief Justice then responded with a statement of his interpretation of the law at that time, which went straight to the heart of the key issue at hand, namely "justification":

> "*You cannot be admitted, Mr. Hamilton, to give the truth of a libel in evidence. A libel is not to be justified; for it is nevertheless a libel that it is true.*"

The speech of Mr. Hamilton that followed this challenge from the bench is said to have been so elegant and persuasive so as to have completely won over the jury, to the extent that the jury disregarded a direction from the bench not to pay attention to Mr Hamilton's arguments... With the famous quotation, "*Truth should be an absolute defence against libel charges*", the day had been won for "press freedom", whereas, of more significance, was the establishment of recognition in the US of the proposition that it was a defence to show that what was published, however harmful to the Defendant's reputation, would be held not to be defamatory if it were proved to be true. This was recognised in English common law in the defence of "*justification.*"

It was the groundbreaking case of *New York Times v Sullivan*[2] that brought about a fundamental change in the law with reference to the First Amendment. Mr Justice Brennan summed up the task the Court faced in opening his final judgment by stating:

> "*We are required in this case to determine, for the first time, the extent to which the constitutional protections for speech and press limit a State's power to award*

---

1   See: http://law2.umkc.edu/faculty/projects/ftrials/zenger/zengerrecord.html and in particular the Order for the Public Burning of Zenger's Journals, Order of Governor William Cosby, October 22, 1734 and Bench Warrant for Arrest of John Peter Zenger, November 2, 1734
2   376 US 254 (1964)

damages in a libel action brought by a public official against critics of his official conduct."

The *Sullivan* case concerned the publication of a full page advertisement in the *New York Times* in 1960, entitled *"Heed Their Rising Voices"*[3] which claimed that the arrest of the Rev Martin Luther King Jr on perjury charges in Alabama was an attempt to derail the Civil Rights campaign in the south and that the campaign had been met by *"an unprecedented wave of terror by those who would deny and negate that document which the whole world looks upon as setting the pattern for modern freedom."* The document referred to was, quite significantly, the US Constitution and Bill of Rights, under which the civil rights campaigners had been protesting for their right to live in equal recognition as citizens and to protect their human dignity. In response, Montgomery City Commissioner, LB Sullivan filed a libel suit against the *NY Times*, and the four clergymen who had given their support to the advertisement. Sullivan was not expressly mentioned in the advertisement; however, as an elected Commissioner with supervisory responsibility for the Police Department, he claimed that the article inferred misconduct on his part. He argued that his case was strengthened by the fact that the piece contained several factual errors, which the Court accepted were valid misstatements. An example of one such allegation was an assertion that the police had padlocked shut a student dining hall at Montgomery, Alabama in order to starve protestors into submission. The Court had accepted that the dining hall was not padlocked on any occasion, and that the only persons who may have been prevented from entering the dining hall were those who had not signed up for preregistration at the campus or applied for a temporary dining ticket. There was also significant discrepancy in the claim that Martin Luther King had been arrested seven times, whereas in fact he had only been arrested four times, three of which arrests were not, in any event, during Sullivan's tenure as Commissioner.

Sullivan was awarded $500,000 by the Circuit Court of Montgomery County, and this award was subsequently affirmed by the Alabama Supreme Court.

The New York Times appealed to the Supreme Court, who unanimously (9–0 in favour) decided to reverse the decision of the lower court.

They held that a State could not, under the First and Fourteenth Amendments, award damages to a public official for defamation relating to his official conduct unless he proved *"actual malice"* ie that the statement was made with knowledge of its falsity or with reckless disregard of whether it was true or false. In addition, it was established that factual errors or statements which were defamatory of an official's reputation would not merit an award of damages unless actual malice could be proved.

As a result of this decision the First Amendment now requires that public officials suing for defamatory statements made in relation to their official conduct must

3   Published in New York Times on 29 March 1960

prove actual malice. This decision was an attempt to prevent a chilling effect on public debate, and promote *"the principle that debate on public issues should be uninhibited, robust, and wide-open"* which *"may well include vehement, caustic, and sometimes unpleasantly sharp attacks on Government and public officials"*[4].

The approach in the US has been that the press can effectively *"publish and be damned"*, provided they have not been motivated by malice, with the burden of proof resting firmly on the Plaintiff's shoulders to establish malice, not an easy task in any circumstances.

This landmark decision, in tandem with the over-riding right of free speech established under the First Amendment of the US Constitution, explains not only the dramatic divergence in the libel laws on either side of the Atlantic, notwithstanding such common beginnings, but also the roots of the somewhat belligerent opposition to UK libel laws in the American press. Indeed, it is easy to forget that the US defamation law was grounded firmly on English common law up until relatively recent times. However, it does not explain the intensity of the lobbying campaign that resulted in the draconian SPEECH Act, which is probably unprecedented in terms of the interference by one country in another nation's internal affairs.

In reality, it is necessary to go beyond one nation's constitutional rights to identify the motivation behind what has been, on both sides of the Atlantic, a somewhat unbalanced and one-sided attack on not only the legislation, but also the judiciary itself.

As outlined in the previous chapter, the current clamour for reform began in New York against a background of what has been a fundamental change in approach to the law of defamation and freedom of expression, putting the US legislators not only on the polar opposite to their UK peers, but also at loggerheads with the law and approach to defamation in Britain and Ireland.

Another significant judicial decision developing the law in the United States was the 1974 case of *Gertz v Robert Welch, Inc*[5]. The Plaintiff, Elmer Gertz, was a civil rights attorney in Chicago. The case revolved around a publication by the *American Opinion* magazine concerning Gertz's appearance as attorney for the Nelson family. This was the family of a young man who had been shot and killed by Richard Nuccio, a Chicago police officer, in 1968. The state had successfully prosecuted and convicted Nuccio for the Nelson homicide. Gertz had taken out civil proceedings to recover damages against Nuccio on behalf of the deceased's family.

American Opinion magazine was a monthly publication fronting the views of the John Birch Society, the radical right wing group which campaigned against communism. In 1960's it published a series of articles warning throughout of a conspiracy to discredit local law enforcement agencies with the ultimate purpose,

4   http://supreme.justia.com/us/376/254/case.html at II
5   418 US 323

it claimed, of establishing a private national law enforcement agency that could support a Communist dictatorship. In this context, the Defendant publisher of the magazine commissioned a report on the criminal trial of Officer Nuccio. Entitled, *"FRAME-UP: Richard Nuccio and the War on Police,"* the article sought to demonstrate that the case against Nuccio was a fraud and that his prosecution was part of a Communist conspiracy to undermine faith in the Chicago Police Department. Despite Gertz's fringe involvement in the criminal proceedings, he was portrayed as an architect of the "frame-up" of Officer Nuccio, in his capacity as a member of the *"Marxist League for Industrial Democracy, originally known as the Intercollegiate Socialist Society, which has advocated the violent seizure of our government*[6]*."* The article also stated that Gertz, the *"Leninist,"* had been an officer of the National Lawyers Guild, or an organisation that the *American Opinion* considered to be a Communist front that *"probably did more than any other outfit to plan the Communist attack on the Chicago police during the 1968 Democratic Convention."* The article had been accompanied by a photograph of the Plaintiff with the caption, *"Elmer Getz of Red Guild harasses Nuccio."* This was, of course, all utter nonsense, yet the editor of the magazine had gone so far as to claim in the edition featuring the report that its author had *"conducted extensive research into the Richard Nuccio Case."*

Gertz issued libel proceedings against the Defendant publisher in the District Court for Chicago after widespread distribution of the magazine across the United States and in Chicago. The Court initially held that there had been publication of falsity that was harmful to the Plaintiff's reputation, and it further accepted that, as Gertz was not a public official, the principles enunciated in *New York Times v Sullivan* did not apply in this case. In light of this, the jury were directed that they were only required to decide *how much* the Plaintiff should be awarded in damages.

The jury provisionally awarded Gertz damages in the sum of $50,000. However, before the case was ultimately determined, the District Court reconsidered and decided that the *New York Times v Sullivan* standard did in fact apply in this case, on the basis that the publication, while it did not concern a public figure, did cover matters in the public interest. The Plaintiff was held to be unable to establish *"actual malice"* standard against Robert Welch Inc and the *American Opinion.* The State Court of Appeal upheld this decision. This certainly was not the most clearly decided case to have ever been disposed of by the esteemed state adjudicators.

In the Plaintiff's Appeal to the Supreme Court in Washington, at the outset of his decision, the Judge, Mr Justice Powell, summed up the quandary of the appellate Court as follows[7]:

> *"This Court has struggled for nearly a decade to define the proper accommodation between the law of defamation and the freedoms of speech and press protected*

6   *Gertz v Robert Welch, Inc: the story of a landmark libel case* by Elmer Gertz (1992) at page 3
7   *Gertz v Robert Welch, Inc,* 418 US 323 (1974) at paragraph 1

*by the First Amendment. With this decision we return to that effort. We granted
certiorari to reconsider the extent of a publisher's constitutional privilege against
liability for defamation of a private citizen."*

The Court began its discourse with the pronouncement as *"common ground"*
that, *"under the First Amendment, there is no such thing as a false idea. However
pernicious an opinion might seem, we depend for its correction, not on the conscience
of judges and juries, but on the competition of other ideas.[8]"* Given the wide meaning
that may be attached to the word "idea", it was clear that the Supreme Court
had no intention of splitting hairs over the First Amendment. While affirming
that there was equally, *"no constitutional value in false statements of fact"*; or
indeed the *"intentional lie"* or *"careless error"*, the Court found that the First
Amendment required the *"[protection] of some falsehoods in order to protect speech
that matters[9],"* and distinguished the misstatements of fact in the article, being that
Gertz had been the architect of the prosecution against Nuccio, which they held
would not be defamatory, and the statements of political opinion concerning his
political motives ("Leninist" etc.), which would be defamatory. However, on the
basis that Gertz was found not be a public figure, the Court granted Gertz success
in his action, specifically refusing the argument that the *New York Times* defence
should apply to private individuals notwithstanding that the subject matter may
have been in the public interest.

The case had indirectly introduced the defence of *"fair comment"*, with the Court's
paramount dictum that *"under the First Amendment, there is no such thing as a false
idea."* If the subject of the statement was a matter of opinion, there could be no
defamation.

The precedent was qualified in the 1985 case of *Milkovich v Lorain Journal Co*[10].
This case, which was largely anticipated to provide a definitive test for the nations'
adjudicators approach to statements of opinion in the context of libel litigation,
concerned a brawl that erupted from the sidelines of an American High School
wrestling match. The Plaintiff was the wrestling coach at Maple Heights High
School, Ohio and on 8 February 1974 had brought his wrestling team to compete
with their adversaries in the sport at Maple High School. However, during the
contest a fight erupted involving the student wrestlers and some members of the
audience – the Maple Heights team and their fans had attacked their counterparts
with some people being hospitalised as a result. It was alleged that the Plaintiff
instigated the violence, through the nature of his protests against some refereeing
decisions and incitements made to the crowd. Milkovich, the Plaintiff was brought
before the Ohio High School Athletic Association (OHSAA) to testify as to the events
that took place on that day. Following the hearing, the OHSAA placed the Maple
Heights team on probation for a year and prohibited them from entering the 1975
state tournament. Subsequently, several of the Maple students and their parents
filed suit against the OHSAA for a restraining order on the probation and ban from
competition on the grounds that they had been denied due process. The Plaintiff

8   *Gertz v Robert Welch, Inc,* 418 US 323 (1974) at III
9   Ibid, at III
10   497 US 1 (1990).

also gave testimony in the course of these proceedings as to the circumstances of the brawl. The day after the Court rendered its decision, restraining the OHSAA from enforcing the disciplinary measures, the Defendant, Ohio based newspaper the *News Herald*, published a column by sports writer Ted Diadiun. The article, titled, "*Maple beat the law with the big lie,*" was full of hyperbole and asserted that the Plaintiff had lied to the State Court in his testimony for the suit seeking the restraining order against the OHSAA. There was no question as to the implication against the Plaintiff given the highly provocative and inflammatory language involved.

Despite the inflammatory language, a clear issue to be tried emerged after the action was filed, namely whether the contents of the article were constitutionally privileged on the basis of the decision in *Gertz*. Notwithstanding that the article suggested that the Plaintiff had been guilty of perjury, it was clear that the article was an opinion piece, by a particularly one sided (biased towards the Mentor team) and written by a sports journalist who was given to writing in a sensationalist manner. The Defendant argued that if it was established to the satisfaction of the Court to be an opinion, it could not be held to be defamatory.

The Defendant publisher was successful in the first instance and the action was dismissed on the grounds that it had not been established that there had been any actual malice on the part of the Defendant. The Plaintiff appealed to the State Appellate Court, which ruled that there had been actual malice and remanded the matter back for re-trial by jury. This decision was challenged by the publisher at the Ohio Supreme Court, but the appeal was dismissed in the absence of any constitutional issues. The Supreme Court in Washington further denied the publisher the necessary leave to continue its appeal. Indeed, at this stage it appeared that the key issue would not be decided upon in the action. However, when the matter was subject to re-trial, the Ohio State Court granted judgement in favour of the publisher, on the grounds that the article did attract protection on the basis that it was an opinion and therefore protected by "*constitutional law.*" There was then a further shift on this determination, where on the Plaintiff's appeal, the Supreme Court of Ohio found that the article represented a series of "*factual assertions as a matter of law*" and therefore did not attract privilege. However, the Defendant's application in 1979 again for leave for an appeal to be heard at the Supreme Court in Washington DC was refused. It was only by virtue of a related action brought by the Maple Heights schools district superintendent, an H. Donald Scott, decided in 1986, where the Court found in favour of the publisher on the basis that the article should be regarded as opinion and accordingly be "*constitutionally protected*" that the matter was revisited. The Ohio Court of Appeals for Milkovich's case ruled that it would be bound by the *Scott* decision and again reversed its decision. It was against this background that the Supreme Court eventually granted leave or *certiorari* to consider "*the important questions raised by the Ohio courts' recognition of a constitutionally-required 'opinion' exception to the application of its defamation law.*" Unsurprisingly, it was widely anticipated that the Supreme Court would hand down a milestone judgement for jurisprudence in the area of constitutional law and defamation. The Court's findings, however, were unfortunately much less categorical than had been expected.

In his summing up, Chief Justice Rehnquist, on behalf of a majority of 5 to 2, refused to rule in favour of the establishment of an unqualified constitutional privilege in respect of all publications that could be identified as opinion as opposed to statements of fact. While highlighting that:

> *"the numerous decisions... establishing First Amendment protection for defendants in defamation actions surely demonstrate the Court's recognition of the [First] Amendment's vital guarantee of free and uninhibited discussion of public issues...*[11]*"*

Chief Justice Rehnquist went on to state:

> *"...But there is another side to the equation; we have regularly acknowledged the 'important social values which underlie the law of defamation,' and recognise that, 'society has a pervasive and strong interest in preventing and redressing attacks upon reputation'.... 'The right of a man to the protection of his own reputation from unjustified invasion and wrongful hurt reflects no more than our basic concept of the essential dignity and worth of every human being – a concept at the root of any decent system of ordered liberty.*[12]*'"*

This was certainly a surprising departure from the avalanche of judicial activism held out in almost absolute adherence to the First Amendment principle of free speech. This more balanced jurisprudence espoused by Rehnquist represented what would be effectively the end of the First Amendment charge in the US Supreme Court. The judgement went on to confirm that where there was a media defendant, a statement on matters of public concern, as would attract the protection set down in *Gertz*, had to be proved as false before it would qualify for an assessment as to liability. In the facts of the case at hand, this was accepted on the basis that the allegation of perjury could be proved false by comparing the transcripts for the Plaintiff's testimonies at the OHSAA hearing and the state Court. While it was confirmed that a statement which could not reasonably be interpreted as stating facts about an individual would be protected, the one categoric pronouncement was that the reference to "*opinion*" in *Gertz* was *not* intended to create a definitive constitutional privilege. As compared to the more reactionary decisions preceding it, the reasoning in that case was tempered by an assessment of competing interests – a theme which it is suggested should be vehemently fought for in terms of retaining a measure of circumspection and reasonableness in our approach to the issue of reform in the area of defamation. This approach also reflects the balancing exercise promoted by the formulation of the European Convention of Human Rights, the influence of which in the debate will be discussed in a later chapter.

In the 1988 case of *Hustler Magazine v Falwell*[13], Supreme Court Judge Chief Justice Rehnquist stepped up again to deal with a more unique challenge to the constitutional protection when faced with a suit concerning a manifestly vulgar

---

11   *Milkovich v Lorain Journal Co*, 497 US 1 (1990), Opinion of Chief Justice Rehnquist
12   Ibid at 12
13   485 US 46

yet equally unbelievable parody published by Larry Flint's pornographic *Hustler Magazine*, relating to the Plaintiff, televangelist and conservative commentator, Jerry Falwell. Falwell had sued after the November 1983 issue of the salacious glossy featured a "parody" of an advertisement for Campari Liqueur that included a mock interview with the Plaintiff concerning his "*first time*" – in keeping with a theme taken up in the brand's genuine advertisements at that time. The text would have it that the Plaintiff's first time was a drunken encounter with his mother in an outhouse. With some degree of moot responsibility, the advert also featured a small print disclaimer disabusing the meticulous examiner of its authenticity. Falwell had sued for damages for, curiously, invasion of privacy, but also libel and infliction of emotional distress. The Virginia District Court had ruled that the advertisement was so obviously ridiculous that it could not possibly be considered true by any reader, and dismissed the privacy and libel elements of the claim. However a six figure award was made for the infliction of emotional distress. This decision was upheld on appeals through the State Appellate Courts. Crucially, the Court of Appeals had rejected the proposition that because the advert did not relate to true facts concerning the Plaintiff, it was to be considered to be an opinion and accordingly attract the protection of the First Amendment. The Supreme Court overturned the lower Court's award of damages on the grounds of the Plaintiff having suffered "*emotional distress*". The Court ruled that the publication was not defamatory on the basis that it was so obviously ridiculous that the public could not possibly have believed it to have been true. Chief Justice Rehnquist was once again concise in his assessing the task before the US Supreme Court:

"*This case presents us with a novel question involving First Amendment limitations upon a State's authority to protect its citizens from the intentional infliction of emotional distress. We must decide whether a public figure may recover damages for emotional harm caused by the publication of an ad parody offensive to him, and doubtless gross and repugnant in the eyes of most.*[14]"

The first principle asserted by the Court was that the First Amendment recognised the "*fundamental importance of the free flow of ideas and opinions on matters of public interest and concern*," and that public debate was bound to lead to open criticism of public figures, it being accepted that Falwell did fit into that category. The question arose as to whether this publication could be regarded as having been made with the "actual malice" requirement set by the case of *New York Times*. The Plaintiff argued that, while the publication could not possibly be believed to have been a false statement of fact, this should be disregarded in a case where there had been intention to cause and suffering of severe emotional distress. It was opined that many states had allowed for culpability in these circumstances where the conduct was said to have been sufficiently "outrageous." The Court reflected upon the history and value of cartoon satire in the arena of political journalistic debate before resting upon the following principle expressed by its peers:

14   *Hustler Magazine and Larry C. Flynt, Petitioners v Jerry Falwell*, 485 US 46 (1988), Opinion of Chief Justice Rehnquist, Paragraph 1

> *"[T]he fact that society may find speech offensive is not a sufficient reason for suppressing it. Indeed, if it is the speaker's opinion that gives offense, that consequence is a reason for according it constitutional protection. For it is a central tenet of the First Amendment that the government must remain neutral in the marketplace of ideas.*[15]*"*

The Court ultimately held that public figures and officials could not be entitled to damages for intentional infliction of emotional distress by reason of offensive or "outrageous" publications without showing that the same publication contained false statements of fact that were made with the necessary "actual malice."

This decision emphasised the pervasiveness of the American Court's approach to the constitutional protection of free speech, and was yet another victory for political commentators.

Subsequently, the case of *Stratton Oakmont, Inc v Prodigy Services Co*[16] saw the defamation law in the United States begin to address the new dynamic introduced by the growth of internet usage. Prior to this case, it had been established that an Internet Service Provider (ISP) could not be held responsible for the content of material published on the internet by way of Internet forum[17]. Essentially, the Court had drawn comparison of an internet forum with a public library. Accordingly the ISP or forum publisher could not be held liable for libellous publications made by (often anonymous) third parties on its message or bulletin-boards as they did not have sufficient knowledge or reason for knowledge of the publication of the allegedly defamatory statements. In *Prodigy*, however, the Court had taken a different view on the operator of an Internet forum called "*Money Talk*", whereupon there had been published assertions that the Plaintiff investment banking firm had been guilty of fraud. The Defendant had essentially pleaded the same defence, that in effect it could not be held up as publisher of the offending statements. However, this was countered by evidence brought to show the degree of control that *Prodigy* did have over the content of the forums, namely that it maintained a set of guidelines, made use of screening software for removal of offensive language from all posts on the bulletin boards and appointed members of the forums to act as "Leaders" to regulate their use by other subscribers. The Supreme Court for the state of New York held that these measures constituted sufficient editorial control for the ISP to be held liable as publisher of the defamatory material.

This precedent left the other ISP forum operators in something of a quandary, particularly those that wished to keep their service free from vulgar content. On the one hand, if they chose to take measures to police the content of their forums, there was an attendant risk of being held liable for any defamatory content posted. On the other hand, adherence to the principle of unrestricted use of forums, while allowing for avoidance of liability, left forum operators

15   *FCC v Pacifica Foundation*, 438 US 56
16   1995 NY Misc Lexis 229
17   *Cubby, Inc. v CompuServe, Inc.*, 776 F Supp. 135 (SDNY 1991)

unable to regulate content for the benefit of children and more vulnerable subscribers.

However, in 1996 Congress enacted the Communications Decency Act[18], the provisions of which effectively reversed this decision. The relevant section stated *"No provider or user of an interactive computer shall be treated as a publisher or speaker of any information provided by another information content provider"*. This effectively precluded a libel claim on the basis of internet publication where the contributor was able to remain anonymous.

Again it is seen that the culmination of the developed approach in the US has been that the press can effectively "publish and be damned", provided that it cannot be shown that they have not been motivated by malice. The burden of establishing malice rests firmly on the Plaintiff's shoulders – not an easy task in any circumstances. To the contrary, in the UK, the burden of proof rests firmly on the publisher to justify the accuracy of what has been alleged or to establish one of the public interest or other defences available in specific circumstances. It is this contrasting evidential requirement that forms the basis of the clash between two different legal cultures, notwithstanding the media in each jurisdiction having the same fundamental priorities, namely to be able to report and investigate in an unfettered manner, without fear of libel action, and to also compete with their rivals while protecting their own commercial interests. The rapid expansion of the worldwide web has not only brought this divergence to a head and onto the front pages of the national press on either side of the Atlantic, but has also, apparently, led to a dramatic increase in the number of claims being brought by American citizens in the High Court in London. While the actual extent of this trend is open to question, and will be discussed later, it is universally accepted that British libel laws are infinitely more favourable to a Claimant, American or otherwise, and have long been a thorn in the side of the press.

Although the internet age has resulted in an increase in American film stars seeking the protection of the English Courts, it should be remembered that this is not a new phenomenon, with Americans bringing libel Actions before the High Court in London since, and indeed before, the 1950s, the most notorious being the case brought by Liberace.

In what is often described as one of the most sensational libel trials of the twentieth century, American entertainer, Liberace brought a libel Action against the *Daily Mirror* in response to an article by William Connor (aka "Cassandra"), published in 1956. The article described Liberace as:

> *"this deadly, winking, sniggering, snuggling, chromium-plated, scent-impregnated, luminous, quivering, giggling, fruit-flavoured, mincing, ice-covered heap of mother love...[19]"*.

---

18   47 USC 230
19   "The meaning of 'fruit': how the Daily Mirror libelled Liberace", 26 May 2009, http://www.guardian.co.uk/media/greenslade/2009/may/26/daily-mirror-medialaw

Liberace sued on the basis that the article implied that he was a homosexual – at a time when homosexuality was illegal and still largely viewed as socially unacceptable. After a six-day trial, during which Liberace denied being a homosexual or ever taking part in homosexual acts, the jury awarded him £8,000 in damages plus costs. Afterwards, he famously commented *"I cried all the way to the bank"* (it is now generally regarded that an accusation of homosexuality is no longer deemed to be defamatory – *Rivkin v Amalgamated Television Services*[20] and *Robbie Williams v MGN Ltd. and Northern and Shell plc*[21], save for the inferred hypocrisy that may arise from the allegation).

However, Liberace's decision to sue in the United Kingdom was understandable and justifiable as he had been defamed by an English newspaper. In the case of latter day American Claimants seeking vindication in the UK Courts, they have been doing so against not just UK publications, but also against US publishers who have disseminated the offending allegations within the UK jurisdiction either by way of the internet or international distribution. These Americans have felt compelled to take this action out of necessity due to the prohibitive legal scenario created by the First Amendment and US common law in making it virtually impossible to litigate in their home country. The dilemma facing them is that if they choose not to sue, a UK reader is more likely to give credibility to an offending allegation than their US counterpart, simply because, in having the right to sue, a failure to do so would be likely to lead to the inference that they have not taken legal action because the allegations are in fact accurate.

The argument put forward by the US media has always been that they should be free to publish with virtual impunity, provided a false allegation has not been motivated by malice, and that US citizens should and must accept this fundamental principle, not only in their own country, but also when abroad.

The difficulty has been that in recent years, with the rapid expansion of the internet and with many US publishers distributing more extensively worldwide, international stars and their advisers often feel they must take action to set the record straight in order to protect the integrity of their personal brand.

Sponsorship deals can quickly disappear, because most brands do not want to be associated with wrongdoing, or even perceived wrongdoing. Some of these individuals earn more from endorsements than they are paid for their big budget movies or sporting accomplishments. Accordingly, it is difficult for them to turn the other cheek and accept any damage or fallout from false allegations that question their moral integrity and fitness to endorse a household name product. However, the US legislators are clearly in no mood to compromise or abandon their freedom of speech principles. On the contrary, they, encouraged if not pressurised by an increasingly paranoid media, are seeking to impose US values on other countries.

---

20   *Rivkin v Amalgamated Television Services Pty Ltd* [2002] NSWSC 496
21   Unreported, see: http://news.bbc.co.uk/1/hi/entertainment/4502834.stm

Indeed, the US is now regarded as a safe haven, not just for its own publishers, but also for international internet service providers who are increasingly basing themselves on American soil in order to escape the jurisdiction of the British and other European Courts.

Chapter 3

Increased media attention on defamation and privacy

"The truth is rarely pure and never simple".

(Oscar Wilde)

It is hardly an exaggeration to suggest that the past two years have seen a media frenzy over the libel tourism debate on both sides of the Atlantic. This relatively recent interest in international libel litigation, focusing on the UK in particular, was brought about by an increasing, but still relatively small, number of American personalities deciding to sue for defamation in the High Court in London.

The high profile of the individuals concerned, and the interest their claims have attracted, appears to have created a knee jerk panic in Britain and America, with the press fearing not just a run of potentially large damages awards, but also that the profile of these claims could possibly encourage other lesser known mortals to follow suit.

Although Americans have, as explained in the previous chapter, taken advantage of the UK's more favourable libel laws for many decades, dating back to Liberace's famous case and beyond, there has in recent times been a marked increase in the number of these claims for two very specific reasons.

Firstly, the rapid expansion of the internet has resulted in the extended publication internationally of established US newspapers and periodicals, many of which can and are readily downloaded from within the UK and other European jurisdictions. Indeed, with more and more US sitcoms being broadcast on international networks, it is no longer just movie and music stars who are household names, but also those who have become known as *"B list celebrities"* are now in a position to establish that they have an acknowledged reputation in the eyes of the British public. Another aspect, and the motivating factor behind this type of litigation, is the increasing importance of brand protection, with the credibility of the names of international personalities – their brands – being just as important to their commercial interests as to their professional achievements and personal reputation. Accordingly, a derogatory comment here or the reporting of an unsavoury incident there can have extremely serious financial repercussions for the individual concerned. The international personality is often left with no alternative but to seek vindication in the UK Courts in order to satisfy the moral and other requirements of commercial sponsors.

Normally the first port of call for a defamed celebrity will be his publicist or PR representative, who will undertake a damage limitation exercise in the form of direct contact with the newspaper concerned, which often can be persuaded to retract or amend a story, in return for an exclusive at some point in the future.

However, with the decline in sales of the traditional press, both tabloids and broadsheets, commercial competition between publications is more intense than ever. This has resulted in a media tendency towards taking greater risks and more urgency being attached to the timing for publication. This inevitably leads to mistakes, if not the publication of totally reckless allegations.

The second reason for the apparent increase in international libel litigation in the UK Courts is the prohibitive nature of the incredibly obstructive hurdles facing an individual wishing to bring an action in the United States. Not only do the First Amendment and other protections leave a Claimant with the extremely difficult, if not totally insurmountable, burden of having to prove actual and specific malice on the part of the publisher, but the introduction by States such as California of SLAPP motions, with the various cost risks involved, is discouraging to all but the most resolute and determined of litigants.

The California state legal system's SLAPP motion, which is more specifically known as Section 425.16 of the Code of Civil Procedure was introduced to counter what the Californian Legislature determined to be *"a disturbing increase in lawsuits brought primarily to chill the valid exercise of constitutional rights of freedom of speech and petition for the redress of grievances"*[1]. Such lawsuits had been dubbed "Strategic Lawsuits Against Public Participation" or SLAPPs.

Some commentators allege that the vast majority of SLAPP suits are unlikely to succeed on the merits and are brought in order to intimidate individuals from speaking out on a public issue. In cases involving the public interest, free speech or petition rights, the anti SLAPP statute gives a Defendant the opportunity to file a special motion to strike out a complaint and automatically freeze the discovery process unless the Plaintiff can demonstrate that he is likely to prevail in his underlying claim. As a result, the burden of proof on the Plaintiff is onerous, and, it could be said, unfair, as it effectively asks the Plaintiff to prove his case and establish the presence of actual malice, before he is permitted the usual access to background documentation that he may be aware will be essential to his case. On the other hand, if the Defendant succeeds in having the complaint struck out, the Plaintiff will be exposed to mandatory liability for legal costs, even before his case is "off the ground".

While there is currently no Federal Anti-SLAPP legislation, a growing number of states have followed California's example and enacted similar legislation.

Although a number of defamation Actions have been successfully prosecuted in the US, given that costs rarely follow the event in that jurisdiction, only in the most

---

1   CAL CCP CODE § 425.16: California Code – Section 425.16

exceptional cases can a litigant hope to come out of what is an extremely intense process that is loaded in favour of the wealthy publisher, financially unscathed. Accordingly, the UK Courts have tended to offer the best, if not the only, option for a US celebrity to secure vindication of their reputation, provided of course that he has a known reputation in Britain and that there has been publication within the jurisdiction. In reality it is only the international figure with a global reputation who will be well enough known to satisfy the former criteria, and this contributes to the media presentation of it as the UK's more favourable libel laws benefitting only the rich and famous.

Again, contrary to the impression given in the media, the Courts do apply very strict criteria in determining whether these fundamental requirements have been met, and that is even before the question of liability, never mind damages, comes to be considered.

Although the number of such international claims are in fact relatively few, the fame of the Claimant tends to result in extensive press coverage, albeit accompanied by the usual criticism of "libel tourism". Indeed, if the press coverage were to be believed, one could be forgiven for thinking that libel tourists were descending on the UK Courts like locusts.

Such hyperbole is distinctly at odds with the view of Mr Justice Eady, who has for many years presided over the London libel courts. He has expressed the view that, far from being in need of the urgent reform that the UK media has recently been clamouring for, our laws have developed incrementally in order to deal with the issues that have arisen in response to technological advances in global media as they arise. Eady J has also publicly indicated that judges dealing with these types of cases are not in fact aware of any such foreign infiltration but rather are only aware of the phenomena as a result of what they read in the papers. It is indeed a worrying attribute of the UK media that they see fit to generate such hysteria when the sources of the purported story are in fact at a loss as to what the fuss is all about.

Notwithstanding Mr Justice Eady's remarks, a number of high profile American personalities have successfully brought cases before the UK Courts including:

1. **Arnold Schwarzenegger** – The actor and former Governor of California had filed a libel suit in the UK against author Wendy Leigh in relation to an unflattering portrayal of him in an unauthorised biography published in 1990, entitled *"Arnold: an Unauthorized Biography"*. The book included an allegation that Schwarzenegger had held Nazi views early in his life. While his father, Gustav was historically confirmed to be a member of the Nazi party, the *Terminator* star felt obliged to file a London libel action against Leigh in 1993[2].

2. **Jennifer Aniston** – The former *Friends* star resorted to legal action against the *Daily Sport* tabloid newspaper after they had published photographs of her

---

2   Unreported, see: http://www.telegraph.co.uk/news/worldnews/northamerica/usa/7915063/US-law-to-counter-libel-tourism-in-British-courts.html

sunbathing, which she claimed were taken while she was in the backyard of her Los Angeles home in 1999 – the photographer having scaled an eight-foot wall and utilised a telescopic lens to obtain the "topless" shots. There were also photographs taken while the Hollywood star was on a private beach in Mexico. Aniston's London lawyer settled the case for a reported £40,000 in damages[3]. The actress also succeeded in winning substantial damages, a reported $550,000, from the photographer involved, Francois Navarre, by taking action in the US for invasion of privacy, trespass and misappropriation of her name and likeness. It was also reported that other American publications that had published similar photographs had also settled her claims[4].

3. **Don King** – The famous American boxing promoter, who also promoted a number of British boxing legends such as Frank Bruno, Chris Eubank, Nigel Benn, Prince Naseem Hamed and Lennox Lewis, sued a New York attorney who had also been acting for Lewis and his company, Lion Promotions, in an unrelated dispute involving Mike Tyson and his promoters (this action involved alleged interference with Tyson's contracts). King's attorney, Judd Burstein had been using the Internet to promote his clients' cause in the course of the dispute and on 8 May 2003 he posted all of the Court pleadings on the forum of the website boxingtalk. com. Consequently, the *Sun* tabloid used the content of the Court documents to publicise the dispute in a typically sensationalist fashion[5], as well as lending a sympathetic point of view on behalf of Lewis. On 5 July 2003 internet debate continued following the publication of an article in the *New York Daily News*, quoting certain remarks made by Don King.

King took action against Burstein in the High Court in London, although he faced a challenge as Burstein appealed the Court's decision to allow King to serve the proceedings that had been issued in London, in the jurisdiction of the United States. This resulted in Mr Justice Eady considering the case in some detail, before ruling that King would be entitled to serve proceedings in the US. The challenge had been based on the argument that, while King's reputation was of course sufficient that it could be damaged as a result of such remarks being published in the UK, the global nature of the Internet made it impossible to distinguish the extent of publication in the UK specifically, as against readers in the Plaintiff's own jurisdiction in New York, where, it had been said, such an action would not "survive".[6]

However, following a review of authorities on the subject, Eady J re-confirmed that each publication constituted a separate libel or *tort* (wrongdoing) and, therefore the libel could just as easily occur in England – by a UK user accessing the website – as it could in the United States. However, the questions of the likelihood of widespread publication and the degree of reputation the plaintiff would enjoy in the jurisdiction became almost coterminous, given the propensity for internet hits to be connected with the subject's popularity in the given jurisdiction. The

---

3   Unreported, see: http://www.guardian.co.uk/media/2003/jul/11/pressandpublishing.privacy
4   "Aniston settles Topless Photos Lawsuit", 21 November 2003, http://www.people.com/people/ article/0,,627087,00.html
5   The Court report describes the headline: "Sworn affidavits list the lid off the dark side of boxing"
6   *Lewis v King* [2004] EWCA Civ 1392

Court had discretion to permit the action to be carried on against the American defendant, and Eady J concluded:

> *"...in an Internet case the court's discretion will tend to be more open-textured than otherwise; for that is the means by which the court may give effect to the publisher's choice of a global medium. But, as always, every case will depend upon its own circumstances.*[7]*"*

Eady J further held that, notwithstanding that the effect of the differences between the laws in the UK and the US gave the Plaintiff issuing proceedings here an advantage, this should not be considered before the Court had reached a decision as regards to whether England was an "appropriate" forum – ie taking into account the above considerations such as publication, reputation etc. The Judge held that this question could be considered after the Court had reached its decision regarding appropriateness. The overall effect of the Court's reasoning was essentially to open the gates to American claimants suing on the basis of general internet publication. King was granted leave to proceed against Burstein in London, notwithstanding the fact that the latter resided in the United States.

4. **Justin Timberlake** – In August 2005 representatives for the former *Nsync singer, and now established actor, issued proceedings in London over the publication of an article in the *News of the World* tabloid in July 2004. The story had been based on a claim by British model, Lucy Clarkson and concerned her allegations, which were proven to be false, that she had slept with Timberlake while he was at the time in a relationship with Hollywood star, Cameron Diaz. Timberlake secured a retraction from the newspaper together with substantial damages. In addition, Clarkson agreed to pay to Timberlake the equivalent amount she had received after selling the story to the *News of the World*, as well as apologising for the "*distress and embarrassment she has caused [Justin Timberlake] and Ms Diaz*," through a statement read by her lawyer in the High Court in London[8].

5. **Roman Polanski** – On 22 July 2005 the Oscar winning film director, Roman Polanski received an award in damages of £50,000 from a jury at the High Court in London against Condé Nast Publications Limited, publishers of the magazine, *Vanity Fair*. Polanski's claim related to the July 2002 edition of the pop culture and current affairs glossy, which contained allegations relating to his sexual conduct in the immediate aftermath of the murder of his wife, Sharon Tate by the Manson gang on the night of 8 August 1969. Essentially the allegation was that on 27 August 1969 or thereabouts, the film director had reportedly been observed at *Elaine's* restaurant in New York, making inappropriate advances towards a young Swedish model, after he had travelled back from London to New York for his late wife's funeral. The trial included evidence given in person by actress Mia Farrow, the star of Polanski's famous macabre film noir, *Rosemary's Baby* (1968). The Court was satisfied that the article was entirely false and after the verdict, Polanski was quoted as saying,

---

7   Ibid at para 31
8   Unreported, see: http://news.softpedia.com/news/Justin-Timberlake-Accepts-Libel-Damages-From-UK-
      Tabloid-6870.shtm; and http://www.brandrepublic.com/news/492274/News-World-pays-damages-
      Justin-Timberlake-libel/

"it goes without saying that, whilst the whole episode is a sad one, I am obviously pleased with the Jury's verdict today. Three years of my life have been interrupted. Three years within which I have had no choice but to re-live the horrible events of August 1969, the murders of my wife, my unborn child and my friends. Many untruths have been published about me, most of which I have ignored but the allegation that was printed in the July 2002 edition of Vanity Fair could not go unchallenged.[9]"

What was perhaps more intriguing in the case was that Polanski had to appeal to the House of Lords[10] for his right to give evidence by way of video link from his residence in France. This was due to his being wanted by US authorities in connection with the crime of having committed unlawful sexual intercourse with a 13 year old girl, to which he had pleaded guilty in August 1977 in California; notwithstanding his plea, before sentencing, Polanski had fled back to his home in France. Under French law he was not liable to be extradited back to the United States; however, had he entered the United Kingdom, he would have been liable for extradition. On the basis of not depriving Mr Polanski of his right to pursue justice unhindered, Mr Justice Eady had granted Polanski the right to the video link by order on 9 October 2003[11]. The publisher however appealed to the Court of Appeal, who overruled this direction on the basis that it could not countenance, or indeed facilitate, Mr Polanski as litigant to escape the normal process of law. There being no other reason than the risk that Polanski would be returned to the States to face the consequences of his previous crime, the Court of Appeal held that allowing Mr Polanski to testify from France would undermine this policy. The House of Lords, however, in the first instance considered that Mr Justice Eady had not overstepped his procedural boundaries in making his original Order, and indeed that the libel action itself was a fair and proper action on the part of the Plaintiff, Polanski. The House of Lords accepted the reality that if Polanski was not permitted to give evidence by video link, he would likely discontinue the action or have his case prejudiced by his being unwilling to give oral evidence at trial in the United Kingdom. While the Lords acknowledged the importance of the public policy consideration of not facilitating evasion of legal process, it found that ignoring the consequences of not permitting alternative means of giving evidence, could also result in irregularity in the law or indeed a breach of the parties' rights under Article 6 of the European Convention of Human Rights. The House of Lords recognised that the proposition of permitting the video link was based on an entirely unattractive principle. However, Mr Polanski's previous crime was not an impingement of the rule of law in the same jurisdiction in which the libel case was proceeding. If Mr Polanski was in effect a fugitive from the law, denying him the right to a procedural remedy to overcome practical difficulties arising in the course of litigation would be to acknowledge a principle that it was correct for a fugitive to be denied their legal rights not connected with the original offence. The option to give evidence by video link, while unusual in libel proceedings, was not contemplated in the Court rules to be the subject of a

---

9   "Polanski wins libel case against Vanity Fair" The Guardian, 22 July 2005
10   *Polanski v Condé Nast Publications Ltd* [2005] UKHL 10
11   The Application was made pursuant to Civil Procedure Rule 32.3 which provides that "The court may allow a witness to give evidence through a video link or by other means"

substantive adjudication exercise. The CPR (Civil Procedure Rules), in fact positively sanctioned the use of video evidence. The permission of the Court for Polanski to pursue his claim and insist on his rights under the civil law was held not to be the same as actively assisting him in evading justice. It was submitted that Mr Polanski would not return to this country under any circumstances, therefore arbitrary refusal of the effect of an available procedure for giving evidence could only be said to be an additional punishment for Polanski's crime over and above the justice that awaited him in the United States, albeit that it did not appear likely that this would be put into effect. This did not accord with good legal reasoning and indeed, Lord Nicholls in giving his part of the judgment stated in relation to the point concerning depravation of a fugitive's rights that *"such harshness has no place in our law. Mr Polanski is not a present-day outlaw. Our law knows no principle of fugitive disentitlement.*[12]*"*

Despite the depth of legal reasoning behind the decision, there was no doubting the superficial sense of hypocrisy and unease that accompanied Polanski's pursuit of justice in the UK in relation to matters pertaining to allegations of sexual misconduct, where the entire proceedings had been coloured by his insisting on remaining outside of the UK so as to avoid the possible risk of arrest and extradition for previous sexual misconduct which he had admitted. After the verdict, the editor of Vanity Fair, Graydon Carter was quoted as saying,

> *"I find it amazing that a man who lives in France can sue a magazine that is published in America in a British Courtroom. As a father of 4 children, one of whom is a 12 year old daughter, I find it equally outrageous that this story is considered defamatory, given the fact that Mr Polanski cannot be here because he slept with a 13 year old girl a quarter of a century ago".*[13]

However, it was still the case that England's finest legal minds had refused to interfere with the important right of access to justice for the individual, regardless of their background or history, where that individual was confronting published allegations which, in that instance were shown to be false, and which had the potential to damage the reputation of the individual that was established at the relevant time. Notwithstanding Mr Polanski's previous conduct, it could not be said that the Court had accepted that details from Mr Polanski's past would impinge on the legal and factual issues in assessing whether a contemporary publication containing false allegations was or was not defamatory. Indeed, it could be said that it was important to ensure that his past, however egregious, was not used as an excuse for further callous attacks on his reputation in the media on similar – and false – grounds.

6. **Teri Hatcher** – The *Desperate Housewives* actress took action against the British tabloid *Daily Star* for stories published in their newspaper on 25 July and 3 August

---

12 *Polanski v Condé Nast Publications* [2005] UKHL 10, per Lord Nicholls at para 26

13 "Director Polanski wins libel case", 22 July 2005, http://news.bbc.co.uk/1/hi/entertainment/4706619.stm

2005, which falsely imputed that she had acted in an irresponsible manner[14]. The same story was also published in *The Sun*, which, following legal action, issued an apology and paid damages[15]. The *Daily Star* was also forced to apologise and agreed to pay "very substantial" damages, (apparently in the region of £100,000.)[16] At the conclusion of the proceedings, Hatcher was quoted as saying:

> *"Anyone who has ever entered a legal proceeding knows that when you are totally in the right, it still takes a lot of energy to move forward this kind of proceeding.*
>
> *"This is probably why more celebrities do not fight back against every made-up story – from who they date, to where they shop, and what they eat.*
>
> *"But when a story appeared about me, insinuating that I am an irresponsible and neglectful parent, I had to draw the line. I will never allow any tabloid to so egregiously attack the area of my life which I give top priority, and that is my parenting."[17]*

7.   **Kate Hudson** – Yet another claim against the *National Enquirer*, this time in 2006 over false allegations published in UK editions that Hudson had an eating disorder. The claim was based on an inaccurate account of the Hollywood starlet being confronted by her actress mother, Goldie Hawn, in relation to this alleged problem, accompanied by photographs of the actress in which it was claimed that she appeared "painfully thin." The tabloid's representatives apologised for any distress and embarrassment that had been caused by the publication, as well as agreeing that the magazine would pay an undisclosed sum of damages to Hudson.[18]

8.   **Britney Spears** – In 2006 Britney and her then husband, Kevin Federline[19], took legal action in relation to defamatory allegations published on the internet and in the 5 and 12 June 2006 editions of the UK version of the *National Enquirer* magazine concerning rumours of a marriage breakup. Within weeks the *National Enquirer* agreed to publish the following comprehensive retraction and apology[20]:

> *"In the 5th and 12th June 2006 issues of the UK Enquirer, we published articles under the headlines 'Britney Marriage is Over!' and 'Britney and Kevin: And Now Their Divorce!'. Contrary to what our articles might have suggested, we now*

---

14   "Housewives' Hatcher to sue Daily Sport", 23 November 2005, http://www.guardian.co.uk/media/2005/nov/23/privacy.pressandpublishing; see also http://www.usatoday.com/life/people/2005-11-23-hatcher-lawsuit_x.htm

15   "Teri Hatcher Gets Apology from Tabloid", 19 April 2006, http://www.people.com/people/article/0,,1184984,00.html

16   Unreported, see: http://news.bbc.co.uk/1/hi/entertainment/4534606.stm; and http://www.telegraph.co.uk/news/uknews/1505652/Teri-Hatcher-awarded-100000-over-sex-lies.html

17   Ibid. 8 (http://news.bbc.co.uk/1/hi/entertainment/4534606.stm)

18   Unreported, see: http://news.bbc.co.uk/1/hi/5198208.stm

19   The couple were represented by the author, Paul Tweed

20   Unreported, see: http://query.nytimes.com/gst/fullpage.html?res=9A0CEEDC163FF93AA25754C0A9609C8B63&pagewanted=all

accept that their marriage is not over and they are not getting divorced. These allegations are untrue and we now accept Britney's position that the statements are without foundation. We apologise for any distress caused."

Never was there such a stark example of time being of the essence in libel Actions, than this case. Only a couple of months after publication of this apology, Britney found that her faith in her marriage had been somewhat misplaced, and the couple subsequently filed for divorce.

9.   **Cameron Diaz** – On 16 February 2007 Cameron Diaz secured an apology from American Media Incorporated, the publisher of the *National Enquirer* magazine. The magazine had run a story in 2005 based on a photograph of the Hollywood star and MTV television producer, Shane Nickerson. Mr Nickerson was married at the time and Diaz was dating Justin Timberlake. Despite the photograph merely depicting Diaz giving her friend Nickerson an innocent, "goodbye hug," the tabloid scandal sheet created a story alleging that the couple were having an illicit affair, being involved in a "smooching session" or "passionate clinch". The publication went on groundlessly to state that the star faced a "grilling" from boyfriend, Timberlake after he had seen the photographs. While the publication in hard copy was not distributed in Britain, it was shown that the article was accessed on the publisher's website from 279 computers based in the UK. A suit was subsequently filed and submissions made before Mr Justice Eady in the High Court in London, before the *Enquirer* legal representatives proffered an unreserved apology in open Court, confirming that the story had no foundation. A written apology was also published and the tabloid magazine also made a payment of an undisclosed but "substantial" sum in damages to the actress[21]. The publisher has now taken the precaution of blocking its website from access in the UK and Ireland.

10.   **Jennifer Lopez** – In 2007, the singer and actress, and her then husband, Marc Anthony, initiated an action also against the *National Enquirer* in relation to an "article" published in the 12 March edition under the headline "*Jennifer and Marc caught up in HEROIN SCANDAL*". The story purported to reveal that the couple had been associated with Hollywood photographer, Michael Star, who had been arrested on charges relating to drugs and possession of child pornography. This was completely untrue. Indeed Anthony did not even know the photographer. The tabloid had however printed a photograph of Anthony and Star together from 2004, although this was simply a photograph taken at a concert where Star had been attending as a fan, and had the photograph taken as a memento. Notwithstanding, the tabloid decided to publish this alongside the article in order to bolster the false claim that Antony and Star were friends. As the article also featured in the *Enquirer's* UK and Ireland edition, jurisdiction was established to issue proceedings against the American publisher, as well as distributors of the magazine in these jurisdictions. Ultimately the case was settled on confidential terms[22].

---

21   Unreported, see: http://www.time.com/time/world/article/0,8599,2082856,00.html; and http://www.exposay.com/diaz-wins-court-case-against-national-enquirer-after-being-falsely-accused-of-infidelity/v/8198/; http://news.bbc.co.uk/1/hi/entertainment/film/6368533.stm
22   "Invasion of the libel tourists", The Independent, 21 August 2008, http://www.independent.co.uk/news/uk/home-news/invasion-of-the-libel-tourists-904111.html; http

11. **Tiger Woods** – In December 2009, amidst the furore of growing public outrage concerning the scandals surrounding the then World number one golfer's personal life, Woods was granted an injunction by Mr Justice Eady[23] restraining the publication of photographs claimed to have been shots of the sports star naked, which had initially been published in the United States. The use of a super-injunction exacerbated the debate over the privilege celebrities appeared to be granted by the English Courts in matters concerning privacy[24].

12. **Angelina Jolie and Brad Pitt** – On 24 January 2010, the *News of the World* published an unsubstantiated allegation that, based on fictitious legal papers, the Hollywood couple had begun negotiations in preparation for separation and divorce, following similar reports that the couple had been having difficulties in their marriage throughout the previous December. The *News of the World* article wrongly alleged that the couple had visited a divorce lawyer in December with a view to coming to an agreement for division of their $205m fortune and creating custody arrangements for their six children. Some reports that repeated the allegations identified the divorce lawyer as Sorrell Trope. Within weeks of the story breaking, and following apparent refusal by the tabloid to publish a retraction of the story, Pitt and Jolie had issued proceedings in London. A statement was subsequently issued that the contents of the article were totally false and a letter was produced from Trope confirming that he had never even met with the couple[25]. Eventually, the *News of the World* publicly retracted the story, accepting that the allegations were *"false and intrusive,"* and apologised. A substantial undisclosed sum was also paid over in damages[26].

In many of the above cases, settlement was achieved at an early stage in the proceedings, and the result included categorical apologies being effectively disseminated over the internet – in other words through the same medium that carried the original, offending defamatory allegations.

An exception, in terms of early resolution, was the Roman Polanski case which created legal history in that Mr Polanski was granted the facility of being able to give his evidence by video link, in order to avoid him having to attend Court in person and risk extradition to the US, which had a longstanding international arrest warrant pending against him.

The US SPEECH Act is likely to discourage claims by Americans against US publishers in the future, but of course claims against UK and other European Defendants will not be affected.

However, these cases illustrate the effectiveness of a result in London, or indeed in any of the Courts in Europe, in securing effective worldwide vindication by virtue of the more favourable libel laws on this side of the Atlantic.

---

23 *Eldrick Tont (Tiger) Woods v X & Y & Persons Unknown,* [2009] *unreported*
24 "Tiger Woods uses English law to injunct new revelations", The Guardian, 11 December 2009, http://www.guardian.co.uk/sport/2009/dec/11/tiger-woods-law-injunction-media
25 Unreported, see: http://news.bbc.co.uk/1/hi/8505035.stm
26 "News of the World pays out to Brad Pitt and Angelina Jolie", 22 July 2010, http://www.guardian.co.uk/media/2010/jul/22/brad-pitt-angelina-jolie-news-of-the-world

Of course, European Claimants also face the same hurdles created by the SPEECH Act when suing an American publisher who has defamed them, but several courageous litigants have been prepared to take their chances in striving for vindication of their reputation.

One notable recent case saw Irish ultra runner, Richard Donovan[27], take a libel action against US publishing giant, Forbes[28]. As the magazine's primary distribution was limited to the US mainland, the client decided initially to take them on in New York, where Forbes have their headquarters, but also where it is probably the most difficult place in the world to bring a libel Action – a fact not lost on the publisher. The claimant soon realised that, regardless of the merits of his case, particularly in the hostile media environment of New York, the fact that he would have to discharge his legal fees out of any award of damages meant that on the advice of his local attorneys, he would have to secure an award well in excess of $250,000, just to cover the costs.

Donovan was therefore left with no alternative but to make a hasty retreat, but, not to be beaten, he proceeded to take Forbes on in the Courts sitting in London, Dublin and Belfast. He adopted this strategy, in order both to place the heavyweight publisher under maximum pressure with the threat of a triple award of damages and legal costs, while also keeping his options open until it was clear as to which Court would offer the most expeditious and cost effective result for him in the shortest period of time. The pendulum finally swung in favour of Belfast and, with the agreement of all parties, an application was made to the High Court of Justice in Northern Ireland to accept jurisdiction for all distribution within both the UK and Ireland. Regrettably, we shall never know how a Belfast jury would have assessed this situation, as Forbes finally agreed to pay Richard Donovan £140,000 as a mark of their regret for publishing the defamatory allegations, albeit without any admission of liability. Whatever spin may be put on this settlement, the end result provided Richard Donovan with the comprehensive vindication he had been seeking from the outset, and the case was subsequently the subject of a BBC documentary, as was another successful libel Action brought against a US media corporation.

In that case, the Claimant was Uri Geller, who had been the subject of a false allegation by Dr Arnold Klein, during the course of the Larry King live show on CNN. Klein had made the unfounded allegation that Geller had personally benefited financially from the interview he had arranged for the late Michael Jackson with Martin Bashir. Although CNN had broadcast a limited clarification shortly after the offending broadcast, they had steadfastly refused to do so in the clear and categorical terms that were required to vindicate Geller's reputation. The claim was ultimately resolved on confidential terms, as so many of the Actions involving US companies tend to be.

In an ideal world, many of the contentious issues arising between the US and the UK in particular, could perhaps be avoided, if each nation were to respect each

27   Richard was represented by the author, Paul Tweed
28   Case No 2007 069127, unreported

other's laws. The same could be said if publishers, in the international age of the internet, recognised and accepted that if they are going to profit from the sales or distribution of their product in another country, then they ought to respect that country's laws. Instead, we have a situation where the US are seeking to impose their standards on the rest of the world, and in the UK in particular, notwithstanding the absence of other balancing laws, particularly in relation to privacy, that may be present in one jurisdiction but not the other.

For instance, in France and Italy, the strict and robust privacy laws have almost made the defamation suit redundant. However in the UK, there is no law of privacy as such, and even in Ireland, where there is a constitutional right to privacy, the approach of the Courts remains, to a large extent, uncertain and the implementation of Article 8 of the ECHR tends to be somewhat inconsistent and adjudged on a case by case basis.

Having said all this, the number of Americans bringing libel proceedings in the UK Courts is extremely limited[29] in circumstances where they still face significant hurdles under UK libel laws, which are vigorously scrutinised by the judiciary. As outlined above, the potential Claimant must establish a reputation and publication within the UK jurisdiction, and in doing so, it is not necessarily an easy task to establish, at least in the early stage of litigation, that there had been a meaningful number of "hits" on a specific web page, let alone that ultimately the Claimant's reputation has been adversely affected as a result.

And of course there is the cost of such proceedings to consider. A Hollywood star can afford to take the financial risk of litigation, which is certainly not for widows and orphans. Without a willing solicitor and the law allowing a conditional fee agreement (CFA) and some form of insurance protection, the ordinary man on the street faces a daunting, if not impossible, challenge in this respect. In many ways, the Hollywood star is carrying the standard and standing up against the one sided freedom of speech often claimed by the press.

Investigative journalism in the public interest is one thing which we all must cherish and protect, but scurrilous rumour mongering and prurient gossip intended to undermine the subject is a completely different matter.

In reality, the cases that reach a full blown Court hearing are few and far between, not just those involving international personalities, but also for ordinary members of the public. When do you last recall a major movie star giving evidence in the witness box in a defamation Action? Most of these individuals are satisfied if they can get an early retraction and vindication of their reputation and have no interest in protracted litigation. However, in my experience the problem often lies with a stubborn editor or unrepentant journalist, who on a point of "principle", misguided or otherwise, is determined to fight the case to the bitter end with the resultant increase in legal costs. Then of course when the case goes pear shaped, there is

---

29 Sweet and Maxwell have calculated that in 2009–2010 only three cases could be classified as 'libel tourism' http://www.sweetandmaxwell.co.uk/content/HomePage/SM%20-%20Jump%20in%20defamation %20cases.pdf

an immediate outcry about excessive legal costs, and yet another period of angry reporting in the press with the accompanying clamour for reform.

In the same way that many tabloids are reluctant to let the facts get in the way of a good story, the more respected broadsheets similarly are reluctant to let the actual statistics get in the way of a good campaign. The statistics speak for themselves in establishing that not only are international libel claims few in number, but equally that there are only a comparatively modest number of claims brought by the ordinary man on the street who remains, to all intents and purposes, fair game in the constant and competitive battle on the part of the press to increase their sales.

Chapter 4

The clamour for reform

"Whoever is careless with the truth in small matters cannot be trusted with important matters"

(Albert Einstein)

Having reviewed the background to this debate, we now come to the question as to why there been such an outcry in the press over UK libel laws in recent years. In the past, while there has been the occasional outburst relating to what was perceived to have been an excessive award to some celebrity, the criticism was essentially restricted to reporting on that particular case rather than an extensive campaign against the law itself. In fact, most of the very large awards were made in the 1990s and the criticism was fairly muted by today's standards, with the press seizing the opportunity to get a banner headline about the result rather than the so called unfairness of it all.

In order to understand how such a strong momentum was created, which triggered successive Parliamentary reviews and led to the sidelining of one of the UK's most eminent judges, Mr Justice Eady, we must look again at the *Ehrenfeld* decision[1].

While the case itself attracted little publicity at the time, Dr Ehrenfeld's subsequent publicity campaign quickly gained momentum in seeking to undermine English libel law, while at the same time convincing the media that the circumstances were right for an all out attack on the legislation.

As previously discussed, Ehrenfeld had little difficulty in garnering political support, from the media and political establishment, albeit only after she had failed in her attempts to persuade the State and Federal Courts to grant a Declaration in her favour.

In the meantime, with the Chairman of the House of Representatives' Judicial Committee, Senator Cohen, firmly behind her, and the involvement of a top Washington PR company, together with the might of the US publishing associations, it was not long before further legislation hurtled through Congress, culminating in the signing into law by President Obama. Needless to say the US press was very satisfied with this development.

---

1   *Bin Mahfouz & ors v Ehrenfeld & anor* [2005] EWHC 1156 (QB): see discussion in Chapter 1

However, it was not long before their attention turned to the UK, with their colleagues on this side of the Atlantic enthusiastically adopting a similar lobbying campaign, supported by intense coverage in the print media. Suddenly, we had the last Labour Government and the current Conservative/Lib Dem coalition falling over themselves to keep libel law reform at the top of the political agenda.

However, while this impressive media campaign may have triggered the outcry against the defamation legislation, the question is whether there is, in fact, an underlying need for a change in the law, if not the attitude of the Courts? Putting aside the libel tourism debate, which has to all intents and purposes been undermined with the statistics highlighted in an earlier chapter, is there a need to liberalise the law, and if so, what impact is this likely to have on the rapidly developing internet and the strategic decision of most ISPs to locate abroad?

Accordingly, the question we all have to ask ourselves, as our own legislation has come under ongoing critical review by successive Governments, is whether we want to create the same unfettered approach in our press and publishing industry as that perpetuated by some of the more notorious US tabloids, which are becoming more and more available on our supermarket shelves. This would in effect be to allow the press to disregard any responsibility as custodians of the truth, which has, in my view historically ensured that our broadsheet press has, for the most part, been among the most reputable publishers of newsprint worldwide. For an industry which is subject to the much maligned system of self regulation, the law of defamation has stood as the critical means of regulation and maintenance of standards in the increasingly competitive marketplace.

A number of proposed amendments to UK libel law may perhaps have some merit, particularly those intended to clarify the existing common law. Such changes include the abolition of jury trials in most instances together with reinforced protection for journalists and publishers who can show that they have acted honestly and responsibly. The emphasis is very much placed upon reducing the cost of libel proceedings and providing a clear framework to protect reputations on the one hand and freedom of speech on the other.

However, these changes are arguably by and large at the instigation and in favour of the publisher, which is perhaps unfortunate given that the ordinary man on the street is already facing many insurmountable financial and other hurdles before he can even contemplate bringing a libel action. Accordingly, while we have read much in the press about UK libel laws being no more than a tool for the "rich and powerful" to keep details of their various scandals out of the public eye, the plight of the general public at large is often conveniently overlooked.

We have read much in the press about the supposed abuse of our legal system by *libel tourists* and how our defamation laws are purportedly turning us into an international "laughing stock". However, the question has to be asked as to whether this is simply a convenient propaganda exercise on the part of the media to protect their own financial interests, particularly as this theme has now been expanded to focus on what has become a "national bogey man" – the *super-injunction*.

A super-injunction has been described as either a "gagging order" or a practical protection of a victim's privacy, depending on whether you are a newspaper editor or the victim of a press exposé. What is, however, often overlooked, is that many of these super-injunctions have been granted to people in circumstances where there is a background of a threat to life, blackmail or the interests of young children at stake. Accordingly, while you may find it offensive that a celebrity footballer should be able to use his financial wealth to suppress stories of an affair, from not only the public at large but also his wife and family, it should nonetheless also be borne in mind that for every celebrity case of this nature there are an equal number of very deserving cases where the injunction offers the last line of defence. Just as the statistics have proven that cases of libel tourism are few in number, then we may also find, notwithstanding the high profile nature of some of these injunctions, that the actual numbers involved are comparatively small (a total figure of 30 has been quoted in the press).

Nonetheless, with the same paranoia that accompanied the media's assault on libel tourism, we are now finding ourselves engulfed in dramatic headline articles clamouring for Parliamentary intervention into what some newspapers and MPs are claiming to be inappropriate interference by the judiciary. Indeed, we have had one MP actually demanding that judges should be *imprisoned* if they dare to grant a super-injunction on the grounds that they are supposedly undermining the will of Parliament.

Many of course are asking what the press have got to fear from UK libel laws if they stick to reporting the truth, having undertaken appropriate investigations prior to publication? Is it fair to expect that a victim of a savage front page article which turns out to be unfounded should have to be content with a postage stamp apology beside the obituary column? How many front page apologies have we seen over the years?

And now we turn to the equally controversial battleground of privacy and confidentiality. The same pattern is beginning to emerge, with a stark contrast between the more reasoned analysis in the broadsheets and the more hysterical and paranoid outbursts in the tabloids, with some sections of the press now apparently believing that it is in the public interest that virtually everything that goes on behind closed doors should be fair game. In the same way that the term "freedom of speech" has a different interpretation depending on your point of view, the right to privacy is also subject to a different interpretation, depending not only on the level of your profile in society, but also as to whether your actions have or have not attracted the interest of the media. Equally, we as a society have to decide whether we wish to safeguard our own personal privacy, and as an inevitable consequence afford similar protection for those international personalities whose personal lives remain of such interest to the public at large, or whether we wish to follow the French example of offering blanket protection for everyone's private life. While this is not a straightforward call, clarity on the issue is absolutely essential. Such a requirement is particularly called for in an age where the press are continually pushing the boundaries of privacy to the limit.

For instance, one particular Sunday newspaper believes there is nothing wrong in chartering a helicopter to transport one of its photographers to take aerial photographs of family homes, pointing out where they keep their art collection or their cars, in reckless disregard for the family's safety and security. Such conduct effectively creates a "burglar's charter", and with no realistic financial deterrent the tabloid press have absolutely no compunction in publishing such photographs.

A further paradox arises in the difficulty faced by individuals attempting to restrict dissemination of photographs of this nature, wherein the very attempt to challenge the publication leads to press coverage that exacerbates the extent of publication of the sensitive material infinitely beyond what would have occurred were it not for the challenge. This has been dubbed the *Streisand effect*, after a case taken by the Hollywood legend Barbara Streisand against a photographer who had taken aerial photographs of her Malibu residence[2].

And so there is much debate to be had and many decisions to be taken, ultimately by Parliament. We as individuals have to decide what compromise we are prepared to accept in deciding whether to fetter the media, which has been and remains such an integral part of our daily life and our primary source of information and opinion. At the same time, the traditional press is continuing to come under increasing pressure from rapidly developing internet blog sites and from the need to retain their advertising and increase their circulation figures for their very survival. We therefore have to decide where the balance lies between reputational protection and personal privacy on the one hand and freedom of speech and the integrity of our national press on the other. Perhaps the internet has highlighted one particular anomaly which does need to be addressed, or at least clarified. In the past, a defamatory allegation would typically be published on one occasion, either in a daily newspaper or within the pages of a book. The problem with the internet is that an allegation remains out there potentially in perpetuity, and although you have only one year from the date of publication in which to bring a libel Action, that year runs from the date of each and every subsequent publication. In the case of the internet therefore this could be years after the original posting, as much of the information distributed online is cached or retained in the archives of websites indefinitely. Accordingly, there has been much debate over whether there should be a "single publication rule", which would mean that there would be only one cause of action from the date of the original posting.

This is an argument that has already been accepted in Ireland and included in the Defamation Act 2009[3], with section 11 providing:

(1) Subject to *subsection (2)*, a person has one cause of action only in respect of a multiple publication.

(2) A court may grant leave to a person to bring more than one defamation action in respect of a multiple publication where it considers that the interests of justice so require.

---

2   *Streisand v Adelman et al*, California Superior Court; Case SC077257
3   Available at http://www.irishstatutebook.ie/pdf/2009/en.act.2009.0031.pdf

(3) In this section "multiple publication" means publication by a person of the same defamatory statement to 2 or more persons (other than the person in respect of whom the statement is made) whether contemporaneously or not.

At least this amendment to the earlier 1961 legislation provides some degree of clarity, and it is difficult to mount an argument against such a change, which is likely to be implemented in the UK. Unfortunately a reciprocal change in the law is not on the cards to deal with international internet publishers, who are operating with virtual impunity outside the reach of the UK Courts. The exposure of Manchester United footballer, Ryan Giggs on *Twitter*, notwithstanding the injunctive protection he had granted by the High Court in London, is a primary example of how the on-line publishers are "cocking a snoop" at not only the law, but also the established broadsheets who have no alternative but to comply with the law as it currently stands.

Regardless of the arguments for and against, the ruthless identification of those seeking such protection on sites such as *Twitter* and other social networking forums, has effectively sounded the death knell of the super injunction. Indeed, rather than wait for similar embarrassment to that suffered by Ryan Giggs, the BBC journalist Andrew Marr and Top Gear presenter Jeremy Clarkson decided to unilaterally abandon their super injunction protection, presumably on the basis that to do so voluntarily was a better course than the alternative of a nervous wait for their identity to be *tweeted* in a less controlled manner.

Clarkson perhaps best summarised the resigned feeling of the time when he stated:

> *"One, most importantly, injunctions don't work. You take out an injunction against somebody or some organisation and immediately news of that injunction and the people involved and the story behind the injunction is in a legal-free world on Twitter and the internet. It's pointless.*
>
> *Secondly, you used to be able to take out an injunction and then just sit on it. But as a result of a recent court case you are now ultimately forced by the Courts to go to trial – which is unbelievably expensive. If you win, news leaks out on the internet.*
>
> *There is also an assumption of guilt which goes hand in hand with an injunction"*[4].

A recent and extremely worrying example of the lack of restraint and accountability demonstrated by US online organisations involves the criminal conviction of Sean Duffy[5], a British national who had been using the internet social networking giant, *Facebook*, to facilitate his malicious and highly offensive campaigns of harassment against the grieving parents of deceased teenagers whose friends and families had set up memorial pages as a mark of their remembrance. Duffy, who received a custodial prison sentence and a five year ban from all social networking sites,

---

4   "Jeremy Clarkson: Injunctions are pointless and don't work", 27 October 2011, http://www.pressgazette.co.uk/story.asp?storycode=48123
5   Case number 1100387646, Reading Magistrate's Court, 13 September 2011

had mistakenly thought that his identity would remain anonymous and that his harmful actions could not be traced back to his location in the UK. Such a misapprehension is unfortunately quite common, however, given that it has been widely recognised by lawyers and private individuals alike that *Facebook* and other such organisations, whilst implementing specious methods of alert in respect of harassing behaviour, or 'trolling' as this latest assault has now been dubbed, are almost impossible to contact directly. Standard users who seek to make a complaint about a defamatory, harassing or otherwise infringing post are typically told by *Facebook* administrators that their query is being reviewed and that the appropriate action will be taken in due course. On account of the American *free speech comes first* policy that overrides the entire operation, the appropriate action is more often than not, to do absolutely nothing. It was only on account of the efforts of UK law enforcement agencies and the UK Malicious Communications Act that the victims in the Sean Duffy case were able to obtain some form of satisfaction when justice was eventually delivered in the courts, which will hopefully not only ensure that Duffy is prevented from causing any further distress, but will also serve as a deterrent to other would be menaces who think that they will be able to hide behind the anonymous electronic cover of *Facebook* despite the gravity of their actions.

A further case which is worthy of note relates to the online phenomenon which was for a time known as "*Solicitors from Hell*"[6]. The site, formerly operated by Rick Kordowski, was a platform that enabled aggrieved clients to rate the less than satisfactory service that they had allegedly received from their solicitors. The case is worthy of mention as it caused an inordinate amount of reputational damage and was the subject of complaints from some 100,000 solicitors, collectively represented by the Law Society, before it was finally forced off the internet, its owner now reputedly owing around £150,000 in legal fines. Kordowski has been sued for libel no less than 16 times in recent years and has been unable to successfully defend any of the actions against him. His protestations that the site served a useful public purpose did not impress judges, particularly when he offered solicitors who had been the subject of defamatory vitriol a chance of ensuring that their names were not published in return for a small financial fee. His business methods were not seemingly based on the ethical motives that he held himself out as purveying and as a result he was quick to attract hefty penalties when his, more often than not completely innocent, victims sought judicial intervention.

Whilst the site is currently down, there does not appear to have been any undertaking from Kordowski as to its re-appearance at any given moment in the future, begging the question as to what remedies aggrieved libel claimants will have available to them if he does indeed decide to re-publish the offending allegations. This is certainly one instance whereby the single publication rule ought to be rigorously examined in order to satisfy libel claimants and their legal representatives that the lengthy and expensive proceedings against Kordowski were not an entirely fruitless venture, undertaken completely in vain.

6   *Kordowski v Hudson* [2011] EWHC 2667

It is certainly apparent that libel laws and other legislation relating to the policing and enforcement of what is published online must not be allowed to languish while the world of technology marches stridently on, particularly when individuals like Duffy and Kordowski are so prevalent across the face of modern day internet use.

The Joint Committee on the Draft Defamation Bill, chaired by Lord Mawhinney, considered the complex issue of internet defamation in their recent report on libel reform[7]. The report highlighted the pressing need for reform of UK libel laws to take into account the rapid expansion of the internet in the intervening years since the adoption of the Defamation Act 1996. As expected, the Committee was in favour of the replacing the existing multiple publication rule with a single publication rule which would effectively mean that each new viewing of an online material would no longer give rise to a fresh cause of action.

The report also recommended that a new notice and take-down procedure should be implemented in respect of online publications. It proposed that upon receipt of a complaint, ISP's should be obliged to publish a *"Notice of Complaint"*[8], alongside the material in question, thereby making visitors to their site aware that the article or posting is the subject of a dispute. The complainant may then apply to the Court for a take-down order, on foot of which both parties will be invited to make written submissions to the Court. If a take-down order is subsequently granted it must be implemented by the ISP or host immediately. While these appear to be laudable proposals in theory, they unfortunately fail to address the fundamental difficulty of taking enforcement action against a non compliant ISP particularly if it is based outside the jurisdiction.

However, while the impetus for the campaign for libel law reform can be clearly identified and understood, the question still has to be answered as to whether the demanded reforms are in fact wholly necessary. Interestingly, the press do not appear to have been so fixated on the enormous and apparently disproportionate personal injury awards in the United States, which are more often made up of punitive rather than compensatory damages. For instance, in the well known case of *Liebeck v McDonalds PTS, Inc*[9], the Plaintiff who had been burned by "super heated coffee" purchased from the Defendant's drive through restaurant in Albuquerque, New Mexico, was awarded $160,000 damages in compensation, but with additional *punitive* damages of a staggering $2.7m. However, even this award paled into insignificance in comparison to the enormous punitive damages of almost $80M in the case of *Philip Morris USA v Williams*[10]. This case resulted in the widow of a former smoker taking home the record sum of damages as a result of her successful claim against the cigarette manufacturers on the basis that they had been fraudulent in advertising smoking as being less harmful than it actually was.

---

7   Joint Committee on the Draft Defamation Bill, *First Report* (2011) para 81
     http://www.publications.parliament.uk/pa/jt201012/jtselect/jtdefam/203/20302.htm
8   Ibid, para104
9   D-202 CV-93-02419, 1995 WL 360309
10   549 US 346 (2007).

Perhaps surprisingly, given the difficulties in bringing a libel Action in the United States, and indeed the rarity of such claims, juries have not been too slow to award punitive damages in defamation Actions. For instance, in *MMAR Group, Inc v Dow Jones & Co*[11], the jury awarded over $200m at the initial Hearing, although on re-trial the case was dismissed. The initial award, however, which resulted from allegations that the plaintiff firm drove away its clients, was four times larger than the previous award in a US libel claim. In *Feazell v AH Belo Corp*[12] a District Attorney who had been alleged to have acted slowly in prosecuting drugs related cases and to have possibly accepted bribes in cases involving drink driving was awarded $41m in punitive damages against a TV company. The jury's verdict included $17m in actual damages, comprising $2m in damage to the plaintiff's business, $9m in respect of the damage that the offending broadcasts had caused to his reputation and $6m to cover the personal humiliation that he had suffered. The $41m awarded by way of punitive damages made a provision for $1m to be payable by the journalist responsible for the series of broadcasts. The case, which rested on the legal standard of actual malice, was settled on confidential terms prior to appeal. However a similar punitive award, this time $37m, was awarded in *Bob Guicone v Hustler Magazine*[13] , following the latter's publication of a doctored photograph of the rival publisher engaged in sexual acts in a parody. Again there was a confidential settlement prior to re-trial following appeal.

Certainly, even the largest UK defamation awards pale into insignificance when compared to the aforesaid examples. In recent times, whether as a result of directions to the jury from the trial Judge or the ongoing press campaign, awards in the UK at least have been more measured. Indeed, the general view has been that only the more serious cases should attract an award of damages in excess of £20,000. Nonetheless, there is still a clamour for reform and in particular the removal of the right to trial by jury, or that the Judges should give even more robust guidelines on damages to a jury. Some of the more vigorous campaigners have been calling for the equivalent of a small claims Court to hear libel Actions.

The problem is that, from a Claimant's point of view, it is the very threat of a significant damages award that can often level the playing field in terms of encouraging an early settlement. Without the deterrent of a large damages award, a Defendant will be more tempted to contest a case, perhaps regardless of the merits, leaving the Claimant, already up against the odds financially, in an even more difficult position.

The other side of the coin, from a publisher's perspective, is that both freedom of speech and investigative journalism are severely hampered in circumstances where the threat of a major financial award would effectively amount to legal blackmail. Of course another counter argument would be that if the newspaper is in the right and the allegations are well founded, then they should have the courage of their convictions and fight the case in the knowledge that the Claimant will be stuck with both sets of legal costs. If they are not sure of their facts, which

11   Civ NO H-95-1262 (SD Tex 1997)
12   No 86-22271 (Tex Dist Ct McLennan County, Apr 19, 1991)
13   No 86-22271 (Tex Dist Ct McLennan County, Apr 19, 1991)

they should have been before publication, then they should surely be required to pay the price.

In a perfect world of course, if an innocent mistake is made, then the publisher should immediately be prepared not only to correct the error but to ensure that the correction and, if appropriate, apology, is afforded the same degree of prominence as the offending article. In other words, efforts should be made to put the victim of the defamatory allegation back in the same position he was before publication insofar as is possible. Unfortunately, the issues are never that simple and often the damage has been done as a result of the initial publication and the Claimant will feel that he is entitled to additional reparations in the form of damages. Accordingly, if there is to be a change in the law due balance needs to be afforded to both deterrent and protection, which is undoubtedly a difficult balance to achieve, as can be seen from the considerable level of debate generated from the proposals and consultation period surrounding the changes to UK libel legislation.

The reforms have come under criticism from Claimant lawyers on account of what would appear to be a concerted attempt to limit prospective claims for libel. A primary objective of the reforms had been that all complaints would be subjected to what has come to be known as the "substantial harm" test, at an early stage in the litigation. Whilst perhaps based on logical and commendable grounds, such rigorous scrutiny is unlikely to clarify matters and will instead arguably open up the question of what actually constitutes the acid test of substantial harm. Indeed, the question remains as to whether any pragmatic test can in fact be effective for such an unquantifiable entity. Pinning down such a subjective concept will no doubt further serve to clog up the Courts' time and in so doing increase the fees that lawyers will inevitably incur in arguing their respective clients' positions.

Considerable debate has surrounded the *"Reynolds"* principles of responsible journalism as outlined in the much quoted case of Albert Reynolds, (former Taoiseach (Prime Minister) of Ireland) against Times Newspapers[14].

The background to the case rested on an article which had been published in the *Sunday Times* alleging that Reynolds was not only untruthful but was also a *"gombeen man"*. Perhaps not the most obvious libel, it was still sufficiently damaging to presume that a number of reasonable readers would have understood this term to refer to someone who is primarily interested in financial gain, usually at the expense of others; a more colloquial definition being wheeler-dealer. It is derived from the Irish word *"gaimbín"*, which relates to monetary interest and has been traditionally associated with the money lenders who were said to have exploited the famine victims in Ireland in the mid 19th century.

Whilst giving his evidence, Reynolds was particularly vexed at the fact that the English edition of the paper carried the damaging words whereas the Irish edition did not. He was correct in that the Irish edition differed markedly from that published in England. The fact was not lost on either the Court of Appeal or the House of Lords

---

14   *Reynolds v Times Newspapers Ltd & Ors* [1999] UKHL 45

who both noticed the defendant's lack of explanation for the fact that Reynolds could not conceivably be both the victim of circumstance, as they had suggested in the Irish article and at the same time a devious liar, as intimated in the English one.

The Defendant newspaper was unable to justify the words which Reynolds argued were defamatory of him, nor were they able to deploy any fair comment defence. Accordingly they pleaded statutory qualified privilege, or rather the duty-interest test as it is commonly known, which at the time was the only kind of qualified privilege available to libel defendants. After the nominal award of 1p in the first instance trial, the Court of Appeal decreed that the defence of qualified privilege, as it then stood, was not applicable. The Times appealed the decision and as a result, the common law defence of *Reynolds* qualified privilege came into being.

It was importantly recognised in that case that where responsible journalism had been observed, it ought to be taken into consideration when made the subject of a complaint. In an attempt to delineate the distinction between responsible journalism and what one could only suppose to be irresponsible journalism, Lord Nicholls established a set of criteria that journalists and their actions would be judged by.

Those principles have been enshrined as the *"Reynolds factors"* and they provide a pragmatic and workable set of pointers for journalists seeking to run a story that may result in controversy at best and court action at worst. For the sake of completeness those principles are as follows:

(1)   The seriousness of the allegation. The more serious the charge, the more the public is misinformed and the individual harmed, if the allegation is not true.

(2)   The nature of the information, and the extent to which the subject-matter is a matter of public concern.

(3)   The source of the information. Some informants have no direct knowledge of the events. Some have their own axes to grind, or are being paid for their stories.

(4)   The steps taken to verify the information.

(5)   The status of the information. The allegation may have already been the subject of an investigation which commands respect.

(6)   The urgency of the matter. News is often a perishable commodity.

(7)   Whether comment was sought from the plaintiff. He may have information others do not possess or have not disclosed. An approach to the plaintiff will not always be necessary.

(8)   Whether the article contained the gist of the plaintiff's side of the story.

(9)   The tone of the article. A newspaper can raise queries or call for an investigation. It need not adopt allegations as statements of fact.

(10)   The circumstances of the publication, including the timing.

These common law principles have for some years formed the guidance for journalists when preparing their stories for publication. A key underlying element of the Reynolds criteria is that the list is non-exhaustive. Lord Nicholls applied such a label to the ten point test on account of the fact that he could plainly see no way to create a list of factors that could or would apply to any given instance of common law privilege or encompass all possible scenarios.

Whilst lawyers are fully conscious of the fact that they are perceived as the lumbering tortoise coming up behind the lightning fast hare of technology, their instinctive reaction will be to caution against changes which could further undermine our clients' objectives and also the fabric and structure of UK libel laws that have been developed incrementally over the years in reaction to the changing needs of society.

Clearly the law cannot be all things to all men, particularly in the realm of defamation law, where the interests of both sides are so polarised and diverse, as has been highlighted by the ongoing debate over the legislation and controversial judicial interpretations of the law.

Chapter 5

The developing laws of privacy

"I'm not that ambitious anymore. I just like my privacy. I wish I really wasn't talked about at all".

(Barbra Streisand)

In recent times the laws relating to defamation have not been the only focus of intense media attention. Privacy protection, such as it is, has been attracting similar coverage as the law has been developing, and becoming an additional or alternative remedy to individuals who have been aggrieved by unfair treatment at the hands of the press.

Although there is no law of privacy as such in the UK, Article 8 of the European Convention on Human Rights (ECHR) provides a general protection for British citizens, although its interpretation and application is still very much at the development stage, as more and more contentious "test" cases are brought before the Courts. The lack of UK legislation in this area of law has prompted many media commentators and legal practitioners to call for statutory reform, which they consider to be an urgent requirement in light of the controversial case law that we have seen developing over recent years.

Furthermore, the latest controversies relating to super injunctions and phone hacking have highlighted the need for a balancing of privacy law to compensate for any diminution in the protection being afforded by defamation legislation. While the libel laws in the UK have remained robust and more protective of the individual, the absence of a clearly defined privacy law has not been so apparent. Nonetheless, with the changes and challenges to libel laws constantly being mooted, the balancing factor of a remedy for breach of personal privacy or confidentiality becomes all the more essential, if only to bring the UK in line with other countries.

For instance, defamation actions in France and Italy are much less common, primarily due to their more protective privacy laws which, for example, prohibits photographs being taken of any individual, whether at a shopping centre or a beach. The private lives of politicians have long been vigorously protected in France, as revelations following the recent Dominique Strauss-Khan case[1] have highlighted. In France and Italy, the press "know the form" and are extremely

---

1   *The People of the State of New York v Dominique Strauss-Kahn* Indictment No 0256/2011

cautious as to what they publish about any public figure, never mind private individual. Accordingly, there has been no clamour for more stringent libel laws, as more controversial types of allegations, whether defamatory or not, are less likely to be published in the first place. One notable distinction in France relates to the etiquette which is typically observed by the media once an individual has given an interview disclosing details of their home or private lives. Whereas in the UK such interviews tend to give rise to sensational spin off articles and a proliferation of related press coverage, the French media will not report what was said during the interview without the consent of the individual.

Under French law, while a well known public figure will have a diminished right to privacy, he or she is nonetheless still entitled to the same respect for his or her family life as any private individual. For instance, Prince Albert of Monaco[2] was awarded damages for what was held to be an unjustifiable intrusion into his private life when a magazine published an allegation that he had fathered an illegitimate child.

Another groundbreaking case involving his sister, Princess Caroline of Hanover[3], centred on photographs that had been taken of her in places, albeit public ones, in which she was held to have enjoyed a legitimate expectation of privacy. One such place was the Monte Carlo Beach Club. A number of the photographs, which had been taken over a period of years, included images of her children. Princess Caroline's battle against the publication of the images and her attempts to stop the press from obtaining further images was a long drawn out affair which was full of negative judicial findings in respect of the privacy rights afforded to figures of contemporary society par excellence.

Finally in 2004 the European Court of Human Rights heard decisive arguments from both Princess Caroline and the Member State which she argued had infringed her Article 8 rights, namely Germany. She stated that she had been hounded by the press for the previous ten years despite the efforts that she had gone to in order to try and protect her own and her family's privacy. She made the point that it was impossible to say in relation to the reams of photographs in question whether she had been in a public or a secluded place at the time. She further argued that in any event the definition of a "private place" in German law was far too narrow and provided little or no protection to public figures.

The German Government countered her arguments by asserting their view that the public have a legitimate interest in the manner in which a public person goes about their day to day business, when not on official duty, in a bid to understand how that person behaves generally. They relied heavily on the press freedoms generated by Article 10 of the European Convention on Human Rights, stating that the German Government had at all times struck the balance between the two competing rights fairly. Submissions were additionally sought from the Association of Editors of German Magazines who put forward the contention that Germany

2   *Prince Albert of Monaco v Paris Match* Civ 1 27 February 2007, D 2007, AJ 804.
3   *Von Hannover v Germany*, Application no 59320/00, (2005) 40 EHRR 1

had struck the correct balance, their laws being some way between those of France and the United Kingdom, supporting their stance with the notion that the media's role of "watchdog" ought not to be narrowly defined.

The European Court of Human Rights, while considering the fundamental freedom of the press that is essential to democratic society, specifically opined that such a right applied not only to *"information or ideas that are favourably received or regarded as inoffensive or as a matter of indifference, but also to those that offend, shock or disturb.[4]"* The Court continued by stating that, *"...such are the demands of that pluralism, tolerance and broadmindedness without which there is no 'democratic society'* before reminding the press that *'it must not overstep certain bounds[5]'"*. A further crucial finding of the Court was that the photographs at the heart of this dispute did not engage any debate whatsoever on public or political affairs and related exclusively to the Applicant's private life. Such reasoning underpinned the final determination of the Court that the publication had indeed infringed Princess Caroline's Article 8 Right to respect for her private and family life.

Despite the fact that this conclusion that heralded a new dawn in the age of privacy was reached as long ago as 2004, privacy lawyers in the United Kingdom are still waiting for domestic courts to fully endorse the protection laid down for public figures and individuals in the *Von Hannover[6]* case.

Other European Member States have distinct nuances when it comes to their observation of privacy laws. In Germany for example their particular definition of the concept includes the concept of the "intimate sphere" (including all information regarding a person's health or sex life) which receives absolute protection.

Whilst many governments across the globe have tended to shy away from legislating on the issue of privacy, the commonwealth country of New Zealand has demonstrated that it is by no means an impossible feat. In 2006 the Law Commission of New Zealand commenced a review of privacy law which lasted five years and culminated in a series of recommendations put forward with a view to updating and improving the existing legislation[7]. Whilst the emphasis has been on clarifying the balance between competing rights, the proposed reforms have been made with the objective of flexibility in mind in order to avoid a position where the rules are so entrenched that new technology will serve to make them redundant within a very short space of time.

The example set by New Zealand is one that all Law Commissions should consider carefully when addressing the possibilities of enacting legislation that will effectively codify what is and what is not in the public interest.

In contrast, in the UK there is no "etiquette" when it comes to divulging private information. The PCC Code contains a provision that *"editors will be expected to*

4   Ibid, para 58.
5   Ibid
6   *Von Hannover v Germany* (n3)
7   The Privacy Act 1993 (NZ)

justify intrusions into any individual's private life without consent" but this is rarely taken into account in practice. Editors tend to confuse what is in the public interest with what the public are interested in, the latter usually being the more salacious option and the one that helps sell their product. At the present time it tends to be newspaper editors and, to a limited extent, the Press Complaints Commission which arbitrarily makes this important distinction until such time that the Court is called upon to decide whether a breach of Article 8 has occurred.

Unfortunately the regulation of the press by the PCC – which not only appears to have been somewhat "toothless"[8] in attempting to control the worst excesses of the tabloids, but has shown no strong will or desire to do so – can best be defined as "lax". An explanation may be that, until recently, no less than seven members of the Press Council were newspaper editors, with other members closely connected to the industry, often the same powerful individuals who were determining what was published in the first place with the same commercial and competitive considerations at the back of their minds when attempting to self-regulate.

A number of media commentators have called for journalists to be licensed, much to the disapproval of the majority of those same journalists. It has been argued that journalism is a profession and as such, ought to be regulated accordingly. As is the case with other professions, misconduct should then be treated with either a complete or partial ban from practising, together with fines and other deterrents. While the prospect of enforcing a system of journalistic licences may seem appealing to many, there is a distinct practical problem presented by the internet, an emerging journalistic arena which is increasingly difficult to police. Unlicensed journalists would be able to carry on publishing on the internet, if not in the print media. Until there is some effective enforcement of regulations to monitor and control the internet, converting journalism to a licensed profession is an unlikely development.

It is perhaps a sad reflection on modern culture that journalists are being forced to question the ethics upon which their role in a democratic society is based. It is abundantly clear that a culture that not only allows but encourages prolific reliance on phone hacking in order to glean material for stories, must be addressed from not just a legal or regulatory standpoint, but also a moral one.

Perhaps of even more significance is the fact that tabloid journalism in the UK has become so aggressive in the competitive desire to secure photographs of celebrities in compromising situations, that victims have been forced to resort to seeking protection from harassment under legislation that was originally introduced in a bid to combat nuisance stalkers.

The problem of regulation still remains very much at large in respect of not only harassment but privacy and public interest alike, the main flaw being that the Press Complaints Commission in the UK is not sufficiently independent to properly

---

8   Report of the Culture, Media and Sport Select Committee on Press Standards, Privacy and Libel (February 2010), para 531

adjudicate on the breaches of its colleagues in the print media. There have been a number of arguments put forward recently to suggest that, had there been a sufficiently independent regulatory body in place, then the phone hacking scandal would simply not have taken place. This is because first, the regulatory body would have been fully appraised of a situation in which this unethical culture was so rife, and secondly, they would have had no qualms about stepping in and nipping the grossly unlawful practice in the bud.

Whilst the Press Complaints Commission vehemently denies having had its "strings pulled" in any way by the industry that it was set up to regulate, and will robustly argue that it feels no sense of partiality in the adjudication of cases and the enforcement of the necessary sanctions, it is now largely apparent that this has simply not been the case. In light of the criticism that has been levelled at the Press Complaints Commission in recent times, the urgent need for an independent regulator, charged with making decisions without fear or favour, is now all the more apparent.

An ensuing problem with self-regulation is that there is seemingly no impetus upon a media organisation to sign up to the regulating body's terms. Some critics of the present system have suggested that media organisations need to be properly incentivised in this regard. The possibility of tax sanctions applying to those who fail to sign up has been mooted at length, although is yet to materialise in the form of any concrete proposal. What is clear, however, is that if the UK press is to abide by the rules that its regulator lays down as regards respecting people's private lives, then the regulator needs to have the power to effectively sanction any newspaper, journalist or other media organisation that falls foul of the rules. A good start would naturally be a clear codification of the distinction between what is private and what is not, as well as with what lies within the realm of public interest and what lies beyond that parameter.

The United States, even without the over-riding protection of Article 8, has at least a clear defining line in terms of what is deemed as private and what is regarded as being in the public domain, and therefore fair game for the press.

Notwithstanding the stringent restrictions on would-be litigants stemming from the First Amendment, there is a clear delineation between journalistic content and conduct; the latter being actionable when a journalist's information is deemed to have been gained by underhand means. Similar principles apply to photographs taken in places where there is an expectation of privacy, and the home in particular is considered a sanctuary. Nor is the newsworthiness of the material gleaned a defence to the intrusion, unlike the position in the UK which allows a considerable deal of scope for disclosure of information which is considered to be in the public interest. In the US there is an additional cause of action entitled *"Disclosure of Private Facts"*[9] which is triggered as a result of journalistic behaviour which would be considered to be "offensive to the reasonable person".

---

9   *Restatement (Second) of Torts §652D* Copyright (c) 1977, The American Law Institute. This cause of action is available in a number of US states, however, the elements of the claim vary from State to State. In California, for example, there must be (a) public disclosure, (b) of a private fact; (c) that is offensive to a reasonable person; (d) which is not a legitimate matter of public concern

Accordingly, regardless of whether changes to UK defamation laws are in fact deemed necessary, it is quite clearly essential on any comparison with the balance struck between privacy and libel laws in other countries, that any such changes should be accompanied by clear and appropriate clarification of the law relating to privacy.

Furthermore, the fact that it tends to be only the most controversial of cases that actually reach a full Court Hearing, and the tendency for the media to settle these cases in order to avoid setting an arbitrary precedent, means that the full ambit of potential scenarios are not being brought before the judiciary for adjudication.

Critically, the fundamental problem has been, at least until recently, that the damages being awarded, even in these controversial cases, are comparatively modest and certainly do not represent a deterrent from publishing in the first place. Even in the *Mosley* case[10], when a finding in the Plaintiff's favour for breach of privacy was forthcoming only after a lengthy and embarrassing Hearing, the award was limited to £60,000. Most other awards have fallen in the £10,000 to £20,000 range, if even that, and therefore pale into insignificance when compared to the financial returns a newspaper can expect from the publication of the sensational story in the first place.

The situation has of course changed dramatically with the enormous sums being paid in compensation to victims of the phone hacking scandal, such as the £2m (together with the voluntary donation of £1m to charity) authorised by Rupert Murdoch to the family of Milly Dowler[11]. However this payment has to be taken in the context of News Corporation's desperate attempts to minimise the devastating fallout following the exposure of their criminal practices. The payment of significant sums in compensation had been their strategy even before the scandal had unfolded, with six figure sums being paid to the Chief Executive of the Professional Footballers' Association, Gordon Taylor[12] and the actress Sienna Miller[13], among others[14]. The payments made to these individuals probably had more to do with damage limitation than establishing a legal precedent and future deterrent. However, the payments do at least provide an interesting acknowledgement that breaches of privacy can entitle the victim to seek damages on a scale never before contemplated by the courts. Whether this drain on News Corporation's substantial coffers will be taken as an example, or rather a deterrent, to other publishers, remains to be seen.

The fact of the matter is that newspapers will carry on making the same mistakes and will continue to flout the principles of privacy unless they are properly disciplined when they are found to be in breach. The defendant newspaper in the *Mosley*[15] case, which involved a gruelling two week trial before a verdict was reached, was

---

10   *Max Mosley v News Group Newspapers Limited* [2008] EWHC 1777 (QB)
11   Source: http://online.wsj.com/article/BT-CO-20111021-709386.html
12   http://www.telegraph.co.uk/news/uknews/phone-hacking/8652126/Phone-Hacking-Gordon-Taylor-legal-cost-could-be-far-higher-at-1m.html
13   http://www.telegraph.co.uk/news/uknews/phone-hacking/8512071/Phone-hacking-Sienna-Miller-reaches-100000-settlement-with-News-of-the-World.html
14   Kelly Hoppen and Max Clifford have also settled claims against the *NOTW*
15   *Max Mosley v News Group Newspapers Limited* (n7)

reported to have laughed off the sum of damages that was ultimately awarded in favour of the claimant. In this well known case, Max Mosley, former Formula One Racing boss, was reported to have taken part in sado-masochistic orgies with women who were dressed in military uniforms.

One of these women was less than discreet about her involvement and delivered surreptitiously obtained footage to a *News of the World* journalist. Both the journalist and his editors considered themselves to have a concrete defence of Qualified Privilege on account of the public interest that they felt arose from the purported "Nazi-theme" attached to these occasions. Needless to say their defence failed and they received the aforementioned slap on the wrists.

We cannot lose sight of the fact, however, that there is less chance of pre-publication warning in these type of cases typically because the newspaper has so much to gain and so little to lose by publishing, unlike in defamation where the press are expected to at least put the allegations to their subject *before* publication. Prospects for securing injunctive relief are therefore also lost.

One has to ask whether Max Mosley could ever have been properly compensated for this infringement of privacy and whether, on reflection, the argument ought to have taken place in advance of publication.

Accordingly, there has to be a strong argument for the imposition of exemplary or punitive damages to deter publication, or at least encourage caution on the part of the publisher. Otherwise, newspapers will simply continue to publish without first notifying the hapless subject of their story or affording them the chance to oppose publication, in the confidence that their "scoop" will amass considerably more in revenue than would ever be lost in the event that a claimant would match the bravery demonstrated by Max Mosley and take their case to court and win.

Needless to say, clarification of the law is genuinely and desperately required in order that all parties know where they stand before the "privacy horse has bolted", as once the damage has been done it is difficult to see how financial compensation can right the wrong in terms of a privacy breach. As has been argued in *Mosley*, the key is to ensure that the breach does not occur in the first place: the most obvious relief being a temporary High Court injunction to prevent immediate publication, giving both parties an opportunity to explore the competing human rights that cover these privacy issues.

Whilst journalists and editors have created a furore in respect of what they perceive to be the chilling effects of injunctive relief, they are yet to offer any worthwhile or meaningful alternative that will offer claimants an appropriate avenue to take *in advance* of their private life being completely besmirched and recklessly exposed.

It is also worth noting that to a large degree, the press has also created the public appetite for these types of invasive stories. The media takes exception to the notion of pre-publication court intervention, which they perceive as having a chilling effect on free speech concerning matters of public importance. Yet certainly where the tabloid press is concerned, the injunctions that involve matters of serious public interest could be said to be few and far between. They are much more likely to involve the intimate details of a well-known person's private life and as such, arguments relating to legitimate public interest are perhaps questionable. If the press wanted to be taken seriously in its standpoint on injunctive relief, then it arguably ought to start paying more attention to stories that genuinely do involve issues of major public interest as opposed to those which simply exploit the public's desire for tittle-tattle, (and of course, tend to sell vast quantities of newspapers).

Those who hold such a derisory attitude towards the employment of pre-publication injunctions have yet to offer any intelligent suggestions in respect of those cases which involve blackmail and threats, sometimes veiled, sometimes explicit, to avoid publishing information that would otherwise never find its way into the public domain, and which form the basis for approximately half of the injunctions that are currently in force in the UK. Injunction-sceptics can only repeat their perception of unfairness which is based on the fact that once an interim injunction has been awarded and publication is suppressed for a temporary period, those served with the order have to incur the cost of going to court in a bid to have the order overturned. They would seek to argue that this is unfair and that publication should never be suppressed given that there are, what they deem to be, effective sanctions already in force in the event that the publication transpires to be an infringement of privacy. Those in favour of some form of injunctive relief and indeed those who have suffered at the hands of the press would certainly seek to contradict the notion that the sanctions currently in force are at all effective enough to prevent infringing publications.

Despite the evident need for some kind of structured, parliamentary response to these pressing issues, it unfortunately does not appear likely that there will be a change in or clarification of the law any time soon. An opportunity for such reform was missed following Max Mosley's failed bid to persuade the European Court to require newspapers to afford the subject of an intrusive story a right of reply, and therefore the opportunity to seek injunctive relief, in advance of publication. An equally alarming failure on the part of Parliament to properly address the problems inherent in this area is the seemingly overlooked abuse of parliamentary privilege which has been deployed on a number of occasions to effectively contravene the Court's decisions in cases concerning the balancing of Articles 8 and 10.

In particular, the Liberal Democrat MP John Hemming, attained a considerable amount of media attention in light of his decision to name anonymous parties who were the subject of privacy injunctions under the protection of the cloak of parliamentary privilege. Mr. Hemming's actions have attracted a significant degree of criticism from the judiciary who, having pored over these cases in inordinate detail before reaching a decision, understandably resent the intervention of an MP who has, without knowing or understanding the full facts of the case in question, sought to ignore judicial reasoning and broadcast information that has been protected by the Court.

Perhaps Mr. Hemming's most controversial outburst was his naming of the footballer, Ryan Giggs as the applicant for an injunction to prevent publications of the details of an extra-marital affair. The disclosure served to add further fuel to the already intense media campaign, both in print and online, surrounding this particular order.

Another incident involved a case in which an injunction had been granted so as to prevent a mother, Vicky Haigh[16], from further disseminating false allegations to the effect that her child had been sexually abused by its father, John Tune. Those allegations had been found to be false by two Family Court judges on separate occasions. They had further found that there was no basis to accuse Mr Tune of being a rapist or a paedophile, as Ms Haigh had previously done on numerous, very public, occasions, using the internet to facilitate her campaign. Despite the court having unanimously come to the conclusion that Mr Tune had been falsely accused, John Hemming MP proceeded to name him and to name Vicky Haigh in Parliament, in what was considered by many to be a shameless breach of the Court Order preventing publication. This disclosure led Sir Nicholas Wall, President of the Family Division, to observe in his August 2011 judgment that, *"orders of the court are not made capriciously and any disobedience of them is to be deplored. If a judge wishes to preserve the anonymity of a child and so orders, that order must be obeyed."*[17]

It remains to be seen whether Parliament will seek to enforce any measures which will prevent these types of abuse of privilege on the part of maverick MPs, although a failure to do so will do little to aid the already strained relationship with the judiciary, who naturally abhor these wilfully reckless, although perfectly legal disclosures of otherwise protected information.

In the meantime, and in relation to the general need for the codification of privacy laws, in the UK at least, it appears that we will have to rely on the developing law relating to breach of confidentiality which has been successfully applied to provide some degree of privacy protection, as well as the existing judicial interpretation of Article 8 which has even gone so far as to safeguard false information, as supported by the findings in the case of *McKennit v Ash*[18]. The *McKennit* case is already distinct from many privacy cases heard in the UK Courts on account of the fact that the names of the parties were not anonymised, unlike in many disputes concerning privacy. This is on account of the fact that these disputes usually emanate from a pre-publication injunction to prevent further dissemination of the facts that are considered to trigger the protection of Article 8. Unfortunately for Loreena McKennit, a popular Canadian folk singer, such information had already found its way into the public domain in the form of an unauthorised exposé before she had been afforded the opportunity to object to it.

At the first hearing of the case, the broad classes of information that had been divulged in the book which were subsequently considered by the Court in *McKennit*

16 *Doncaster Metropolitan Borough Council and Victoria Haigh and David Tune and X (a Child)* [2011] EWHC B16 (Fam); *Doncaster Metropolitan Borough Council and Elizabeth Watson and Victoria Haigh* [2011] EWHC B15 (Fam)
17 *Doncaster Metropolitan Borough Council and Victoria Haigh and David Tune and X (a Child)* [2011] EWHC B16 (Fam) para 31
18 [2006] EWCA Civ 1714

included her grief in response to the death of her former fiancé, information relating to her diet and general health, details regarding her emotional vulnerability and lastly a dispute that she had had with the author of the book. The author of the book, a former friend and aide to McKennit, sought to argue that the information was not only in the public domain but was additionally in the public interest. She also argued that her memoirs were an expression of her personal right to freedom of speech.

After reviewing the book, Mr Justice Eady found that the majority of the information engaged McKennit's Article 8 rights. Only a very modest sum of damages was recommended, however, the Judge having determined that the test in these types of cases revolved around whether there had been a degree of wrongful behaviour on the part of the Claimant in order to justify a public interest argument and additionally whether the information itself has already been so widely spread so as to negate any chance it may have had to attract the banner of being "confidential". Niema Ash, the defendant author, appealed the judgement of Eady J and, happily for media lawyers hungry to have some clarity on the UK's stance regarding privacy law, prompted further deliberation of the underlying principles were deliberated over by the Court of Appeal. Finding against the author and dismissing the appeal, the eminent panel found that Ash did not have any story of her own to tell, and indeed her memoirs would have gone largely unnoticed were it not for the inclusion of the material relating to McKennit. Perhaps what is most important about the decision of the Court of Appeal, as previously indicated, is the concept of "false privacy" or rather, a level of protection in respect of material considered to be private irrespective of whether or not it is true or false. Such a step forward in judicial reasoning perhaps represents what has come to be considered as the most helpful authority in terms of bridging the gap between the ever dissolving libel laws and the constantly evolving law of privacy.

It remains to be seen whether domestic courts in the UK will take the next step and follow the ECtHR decision in *Von Hannover*[19]. What is now abundantly clear is that the advances in technology serve to provide an abundant array of tools which pose a very concrete threat to modern day privacy.

One such tool, which has acquired the ominous title of "the drone", is a small and virtually silent helicopter, which has been discreetly fitted with high powered camera and video technology. Originally designed as an aid to criminal enforcement agencies, the drone has reportedly been used by tabloid organisations in America in a bid to gather ever more intrusive photographic material. One would hope that should the introduction of such a tool in the UK come to pass, that robust measures would be put in place in order to avoid the use of such an invasive piece of equipment. A failure to police such technology will open the door to an entirely new level of privacy infringement on the part of the tabloid media.

Other advances include the ubiquitous "Google Earth" function that is now freely available online. As regular internet users will be aware, almost all properties can

---

19   *Von Hannover v Germany* (n3)

now be viewed in detail online with the aid of this, "street view" technology. Google has come under severe criticism, particularly in European Member States, on account of their stance regarding prolonged storage of street view images and the necessary clash that such activities have with privacy provisions in Europe. In an attempt to lessen the intrusion, Google has largely agreed to automatically blur faces of individuals and registration plates which are caught incidentally in their images. Such measures proved to be insufficient protection in Switzerland, resulting in Google being sued by an entire nation[20]. Following complaints from the Swiss Data Protection Commissioner, the Federal Administrative Court of Switzerland ruled that Google must not simply rely on automated technology to blur otherwise private images, but would rather have to manually ensure that they were indiscernible to online users.

Certainly with the rapidly expanding technological advances available to the press, we are now facing a situation where if steps are not taken to implement concrete privacy provisions, our Courts will undoubtedly be faced with having to adjudicate upon a raft of previously untested privacy issues, in order to draw the line between freedom of expression, and persecution by the press.

---

20   *FDPIC v Google Inc and Google Switzerland GmbH* (decision A-7040/2009)

Chapter 6

A decade of press intrusions

*"Relying on the Government to protect your privacy is like asking a
peeping tom to install your window blinds".*

(John Perry Barlow)

Although rumours had been circulating for a number of years, and *The Guardian*
had, to its credit, been tenaciously pursuing their investigations, no-one could have
foreseen the rapid unfolding of events during the month of July 2011. What had
previously been regarded as isolated incidents, perpetrated by a couple of rogue
journalists and a private investigator, was suddenly dragging in senior editors,
and within a matter of days, Rupert Murdoch himself was forced to give evidence
before a House of Commons committee and engage in what was effectively hand
to hand combat in trying to protect his News Corporation media empire.

The phone hacking scandal not only created a worldwide drama, but also added a
new dimension and urgency to the ongoing privacy debate, and that ever shifting
line in the sand that had often been somewhat blurred and transient. The ripple
effect of this scandal has implicated senior police officers, political leaders, regulators
and media barons. In order to fully understand the significance of this crisis we
must first examine its origins and the prevailing background circumstances which
allowed this activity to flourish on such an astonishing scale.

The Press have traditionally been regarded as a *Fourth Estate*[1] in democratic society
whose function is to provide a necessary check on the powers of the Executive,
Legislature and Judiciary and prevent abuses of power. Indeed, there are numerous
examples of journalists fulfilling this protector role and bravely exposing corruption
in the corridors of power. One of the most famous examples of this tenacious brand
of journalism was the investigative work carried out by *Washington Post* journalists
Carl Bernstein and Bob Woodward into the Watergate Scandal of the early 1970s.
Beginning with a routine investigation into a seemingly innocuous break-in at
the Watergate Hotel complex in Washington, these two journalists uncovered a
widespread campaign of spying and sabotage directed against the Democratic
Party which went all the way to the Oval Office. Given the recent scandal there is

---

1   Widely reported that this term was first coined by Edmund Burke

a hint of bitter irony in the fact that most of the spying was conducted via illegal wiretapping and surveillance. Woodward and Bernstein undertook an arduous and painstaking investigation into this misconduct which lasted several years. Their persistent investigations ultimately exposed one of the most dramatic political scandals of the 20th Century and forced President Richard Nixon to resign in disgrace. Their dogged work and skill was forever immortalised in the Hollywood movie *All the Presidents Men* and both were awarded the Pulitzer Prize in recognition of their sterling efforts.

Closer to home, the *Daily Telegraph* uncovered the MP's expenses scandal in 2009. This was a story of enormous public interest which exposed a culture of greed and corruption among some of our elected representatives which shocked public opinion and eventually lead to a number of those involved being held to account before the Courts.[2]

However, in recent decades there appears to have been a notable decline in journalistic standards. As the newspaper industry has become more commercially driven the focus has shifted away from authoritative and moral investigative journalism towards the more lucrative low quality tabloid style publications which cost significantly less to produce and can generate higher revenue for the media magnates. This slide has been further hastened by the rapid expansion of the internet, the growth in popularity of social media and the advent of 24-hour satellite news channels which bombard the public with information continuously throughout the day and night. In order to compete many newspapers have simply decided to appeal to the lowest common denominator. In many cases it appears that the need for accuracy and thorough investigation has been replaced by a determination to get information out into the public domain as quickly as possible to ensure exclusivity, and that all important market share of the readership.

Of course the responsibility for growth in licentious journalism cannot be laid entirely at the door of the media, it being part of a wider social malaise for which we the public, as consumers of this type of material, must be held partly responsible. We live in a society obsessed by celebrity where Andy Warhol's vision of a world where everyone is desperate for their "15 minutes of fame" has become a bizarre and somewhat frightening reality. This fixation is reflected in rapidly expanding voyeuristic TV habits which are increasingly centred on so called "reality" shows such as Big Brother and TOWIE, where fame-hungry hopefuls subject themselves to public scrutiny in an effort to achieve that coveted celebrity status. This is manna from heaven for the tabloid press which is able to churn out limitless amounts of vapid column inches dedicated to the escapades of these individuals. The media's desire to pump out a steady stream of scandal, tragedy and drama in order to sell copy has led to the adoption of increasingly intrusive methods and the more traditional techniques of fact checking and interviewing sources have been abandoned.

---

2   A number of MPs were convicted on charges of false accounting including David Chaytor MP, Elliot Morley MP, Jim Devine MP and Lord Hanningfield. See *R v David Chaytor, Elliot Morley, James Devine and Lord Hanningfield* [2010] 2 Cr App R 34, [2010] EWCA Crim 1910

Given the intense focus on the *News of the World* and News International Group over recent months one could be forgiven for thinking that the phone hacking scandal was an isolated problem attributable to one misguided newspaper organisation. However, the trade in confidential personal information is neither a unique nor a particularly recent phenomenon in the newspaper industry. As far back as 2003 investigations were ongoing into illegal and unethical practices on Fleet Street. These investigations were allegedly launched under the banner of *Operation Motorman*[3], which was originally set up by the Office of the Information Commissioner to look into breaches of the Data Protection Act[4] by newspapers. This inquiry was triggered by the activities of private investigator Steve Whittamore and his network of contacts who were allegedly engaged in obtaining telephone numbers, itemised call logs, vehicle registrations and other confidential data at the behest of newspapers. Various methods were employed by Whittamore and his associates, including blagging and illegal searches of police and DVLA databases. Home addresses and ex-directory telephone numbers relating to a number of high profile individuals, including several Premiership footballers, were obtained from Whittamore's sources inside British Telecom. Among the victims uncovered by *Operation Motorman* were the parents of murdered schoolgirl Holly Wells, as well as Stuart Lubbock[5], the young man who drowned in the swimming pool of former TV game show host Michael Barrymore.

Steve Whittamore was by no means acting in a vacuum. It has been reported that he used separate colour coded "books" for each of the major newspapers.

When members of the Information Commissioners Office raided Whittamore's flat they unearthed vast quantities of documentation clearly identifying those journalists and newspapers that had engaged Whittamore's services. The documentation which was recovered included handwritten records of both legal and illegal requests for private information submitted by journalists and numerous invoices from news organisations recording payment for information obtained. It has been suggested that some of these invoices were even marked as being payments for "confidential data". It is somewhat surprising then that in spite of this apparent wealth of evidence none of the newspapers or journalists identified were ever prosecuted, and although Whittamore and his associates were charged with section 55[6] Data Protection offences they only received conditional discharges. It is arguable that the lack of action against journalists as part of Operation Motorman may have lulled some in the industry into a false sense of security.

---

3   "What Price Privacy?" published on 10th May 2006 and the follow up report "What Price Privacy now?" published on 23 December 2006
4   Data Protection Act 1998 (c.29), London: HMSO
5   http://www.independent.co.uk/news/uk/crime/exposed-after-eight-years-a-private-eyes-dirty-work-for-fleet-street-2354360.html
6   Section 55(1) A person must not knowingly or recklessly, without the consent of the data controller: (a) obtain or disclose personal data or the information contained in personal data; or (b) procure the disclosure to another person of the information contained in personal data.

The subsequent ICO Reports[7] into *Operation Motorman* identified those papers that had made requests to Whittamore for information. However, disappointingly the report simply lists the number of transactions and does not go into detail regarding the nature of the transactions or their legality. This is despite widespread calls for the full details of the information retrieved to be made public. These calls continue to this day, and commentators have called on Lord Justice Leveson to publish the underlying data. Below is a copy of the table as it appeared in the ICO Report entitled "What Price Privacy now?" It will be observed that the Daily Mail is at the top of the table with 952 transactions and 58 journalists, whereas the News of the World is 5th in the table with 228 transactions and 23 journalists. Unfortunately, this data does not necessarily tell the whole story. It does not say how many, if any, of these transactions were illegal, and the data does not give any insight into whether there might be public interest defences in respect of any of the transactions (in instances where an offence would otherwise have been committed). It does not say the time period over which these transactions took place, and the basis upon which the transactions have been identified are not set out.

Certainly we had none of the sometimes hysterical coverage that was given to the condemnation of libel tourism and the defamation laws in general. Perhaps this abject failure to inform the public about what in any other circumstances would be regarded as a national scandal, is yet further evidence of an abuse of the media's conduit of power. Although the report is available online[8] few, if any, of our investigative journalists regarded this as a story worthy of pursuit.

Furthermore, given the evidence uncovered during *Operation Motorman*, questions must be asked as to why more was not done five years ago to address the trade in confidential information. The publication of the report was largely ignored by the media and it certainly appears that until very recently there was a lack of any genuine political will to tackle the issues it raised. Media reports have suggested that the Police Officers working on *Operation Weeting*, the Met taskforce commissioned to conduct a comprehensive investigation into the recent crop of phone hacking allegations, have requested sight of the *Operation Motorman* files.

Of course, over the years, Governments on both sides of the Atlantic have been embarrassed by various scandals. As noted above, the most famous of these was the aforementioned Watergate scandal which ultimately brought down a President and threatened the very foundations of democracy in the US. This example of courageous journalism carried out in the public interest is evidently poles apart from the model of journalistic practice exposed during the phone hacking scandal based on eavesdropping on the title tattle of celebrities, or accessing the voicemail messages of a murder victim.

Closer to home the former Secretary of State for Northern Ireland, Mo Mowlam, was somewhat embarrassed to find that her own telephone conversations had

---

7   Information Commissioners Office reports (n 4)
8   http://www.ico.gov.uk/news/current_topics/what_price_privacy_now.aspx

Publication	Number of transactions positively identified	Number of journalists/clients using services
Daily Mail	952	58
Sunday People	802	50
Daily Mirror	681	45
Mail On Sunday	266	33
News of the World	228	23
Sunday Mirror	143	25
Best Magazine	134	20
Evening Standard	130	1
The Observer	103	4
Daily Sport	62	4
The People	37	19
Daily Express	36	7
Weekend Magazine (Daily Mail)	30	4
Sunday Express	29	8
The Sun	24	4
Closer Magazine	22	5
Sunday Sport	15	1
Night and Day (Mail on Sunday)	9	2
Sunday Business News	8	1
Daily Record	7	2
Saturday (Express)	7	1
Sunday Mirror Magazine	6	1
Real Magazine	4	1
Women's Own	4	2
The Sunday Times	4	1
Daily Mirror Magazine	3	2
Mail In Ireland	3	1
Daily Star	2	4
The Times	2	1
Marie Claire	2	1
Personal Magazine	1	1
Sunday World	1	1

been surreptitiously listened to, with the full knowledge and participation of MI5, which ultimately resulted in her intimate conversations with the then Deputy Leader of Sinn Fein, Martin McGuinness, during which she used many affectionate, and, some would say totally inappropriate, terms such as "babe". The fact that it was Mowlam herself who signed the warrants to have McGuinness's phone tapped added an even greater twist in the tale. This story surfaced in 2003, but related back to the former Cabinet member's telephone conversations with McGuinness that took place before the MP was removed from office in 1999 after complaints in some quarters that she was too close to Irish republicans. The leak itself was made via the publication by longstanding Northern Ireland editor of the *Sunday Times*, Liam Clarke, of transcripts obtained of the MI5 phone taps in a biography that he had co-authored with his wife Kathy on the Sinn Fein Deputy Leader, entitled, *"Martin McGuinness, From Guns to Government."*[9] Both Mr Clarke and his wife were in fact arrested under the Official Secrets Act[10] in relation to the publication, but not before the arrest was made of a former Special Branch officer who it was alleged had leaked the transcripts to *The Times*.

An opportunity to expose the full extent of the phone hacking scandal was spurned in 2006 following the arrest of two *News of the World* employees in connection with the unlawful interception of the voicemails of Royal aides. Royal Editor at *NOTW*, Clive Goodman and former professional footballer turned private investigator, Glen Mulcaire were found guilty of hacking into the voicemail messages of a number of individuals including the Private Secretary to Prince William and Prince Harry, model Elle Macpherson and Chief Executive of the Professional Footballers Association, Gordon Taylor. Mulcaire was reportedly being paid £104,998 a year by the paper to provide *"research and information services"*[11] whilst he was simultaneously running an agency which purported to protect media figures from precisely the type of intrusions he was carrying out on behalf of the *NOTW*.

Mulcaire may have used a variety of techniques to hack into voicemails. It is understood that mobile network providers have, at various times, improved the security of their voicemail platforms. One of the techniques was to telephone the targeted number simultaneously from two different phone lines in order to ensure that the second call would go straight to voicemail. When the voicemail greeting was played, the default pin code for that network would be entered in order to access the voicemail messages. The default pin code was set by the relevant mobile network providers, and it was relatively common for users not to change their pin code from the default. Other techniques included the following: obtaining the direct dial voicemail number unique to each mobile phone, so that it was

9   Clarke, L, Johnston, K, *"Martin McGuinness: From Guns to Government"* (2003), Edinburgh, Mainstream Publishing.
10 Official Secrets Act 1989
11 Evidence given to the Court during the course of Glen Mulcaire's trial. Source: http://news.bbc. co.uk/1/hi/6301243.stm

unnecessary to call the actual mobile number; persuading the mobile network provider to reset the voicemail so that the unique pin code was reset to the default pin code. Once the pin code had been entered successfully, the hacker was able to listen to new and saved voicemail messages.

These activities were brought to light after officials at Clarence House, the residence of Prince Charles, raised concerns with Scotland Yard about how undisclosed information concerning a knee injury suffered by Prince William had found its way into the pages of the *News of the World*. The subsequent police investigation led to the arrest and prosecution of Goodman and Mulcaire who were sentenced to four and six months in prison respectively. It appears that the police investigation at this time focused exclusively on the activities of Mulcaire and Goodman and did not go beyond this narrow remit to examine whether any others had been involved. Subsequent media reports have revealed that other high ranking members of the Royal family may also have been victims of phone hacking. In the summer of 2011, the Prince of Wales and the Duchess of Cornwall were contacted by police who advised that the couple's personal details were found among documentation which had been seized from Glen Mulcaire in 2006[12]. This is, of course, not the first time that a member of the Royal household has fallen victim to tabloid interception of phone calls – in the early 1990s *The Sun* published excerpts of secretly recorded intimate conversations between Diana, Princess of Wales, and close friend James Gilbey in what become known as the *"Squidgygate/Dianagate"*[13] affair. Similarly in the scandal dubbed "Camillagate"[14], extracts of highly personal conversations between Prince Charles and Camilla Parker Bowles were published in 1993 by Rupert Murdoch's Australian title *New Idea* before being re-published by British tabloids.

The prosecution of Mulcaire and Goodman also resulted in the resignation of editor of the *NOTW*, Andy Coulson. *NOTW* made substantial donations to charities nominated by Prince William and Prince Harry, and paid a significant sum in damages to Gordon Taylor in an attempt swiftly to brush this unsavoury matter under the carpet. When former News International executive chairman Les Hinton was called to give evidence before the House of Commons Culture Select Committee in March 2007 he was firmly "on message" in claiming that there was no evidence of widespread hacking at the paper and claiming that Goodman was the only person who knew about it[15]. This was the beginning of the myth, promoted vigorously by the NOTW, that responsibility for phone hacking lay with *'one rogue reporter'*. Of course, it is not known precisely what investigations were made by Mr Hinton before he gave his evidence to the Select Committee,

---

12   http://www.guardian.co.uk/media/2011/jul/11/phone-hacking-charles-camilla

13   http://www.telegraph.co.uk/news/uknews/1575117/Dianas-Squidgygate-tapes-leaked-by-GCHQ.html

14   http://www.dailymail.co.uk/news/article-522508/Charles-Camillas-lovenest-bugged-Diana-inquest-told.html

15   Q 95 http://www.publications.parliament.uk/pa/cm200607/cmselect/cmcumeds/375/7030601.htm

what he discovered as a result of those investigations, or what he was told by his subordinates. Newly appointed Editor, Colin Myler was at pains to point out to the PCC that this was *"an exceptional and unhappy event in the 163 year history of the News of the World involving one journalist."*[16] The Press Complaints Commission provided legitimacy to this stance when their report into *subterfuge and newsgathering* published in May 2007 concluded that there was no evidence *"of a conspiracy at the newspaper going beyond Messers Goodman and Mulcaire to subvert the law and the PCC's Code of Practice"*[17] and furthermore that *"no-one else at the News of the World knew that Messers Goodman and Mulcaire were tapping phone messages for stories"*[18].

Despite overt attempts to sideline this story, by settling the Taylor case out of court and thus preventing much of the evidence from ever seeing the light of day, *The Guardian* remained undeterred and continued its investigations into the hacking issue. In July 2009, *The Guardian* broke the story that, according to evidence gathered by the police, phone hacking was rife within the *NOTW* and thousands of well known figures, including John Prescott and Boris Johnson, had been targeted by the paper. The newspaper also claimed that News Group Newspapers had bought the silence of a number of hacking victims to ensure that the extent of this practice within the organisation was not exposed. *The Guardian's* revelations were picked up by the PCC which, belatedly appeared anxious to establish whether or not it had been misled by *NOTW* in 2007 when their report had essentially absolved the paper of any responsibility. If the 2007 report was myopic in its approach the Commission's follow-up report is almost farcical. Perhaps more in an effort to spare its own blushes the PCC somehow managed to clear the *NOTW* of any wrongdoing yet again. The PCC concluded that there was *"no new evidence to suggest that the practice of phone message tapping was undertaken by others beyond Goodman and Mulcaire"*[19] and furthermore *"there is nothing to suggest that the PCC was materially misled during its 2007 inquiry"*[20]. Moreover, the Commission appeared to criticise *The Guardian* for pursuing this investigation, stating in the report that the paper has *"obligations under the Code requiring it to take care not to publish distorted or misleading information"*[21]. In light of the subsequent developments which have entirely vindicated *The Guardian's* commendable investigative work the PCC have now been forced to withdraw this report and,the Chair of the Commission, Baroness Buscombe, has resigned and been replaced by Lord Hunt. On 9th March 2012 the PCC announced that it was going to "move into a transitional phase" and transfer its assets and staff to a new regulatory body – in essence the end of the PCC as currently constituted.

16 PCC Report on Subterfuge and Newsgathering 18th May 2007, para 3.1
17 Ibid, para 6.3
18 Ibid
19 PCC report on phone message tapping allegations dated 9th November 2009, para 13.2
20 Ibid
21 Ibid, para 13.1

The Commission was not alone in its reluctance to re-examine the phone hacking issue. In the wake of fresh revelations published by *The Guardian* in 2009, the Metropolitan Police declined to re-open their investigation. It has been widely reported that former Assistant Commissioner John Yates conducted a review of the original investigation in light of the new allegations published by *The Guardian* and decided that a fresh inquiry was not necessary.

Such a decision seems even more bizarre given the alleged quantities of evidence which the police had in their possession identifying numerous hacking victims – the vast majority of whom the police had failed to notify. It is unquestionable that the Met like many other police forces is anxious to secure favourable coverage of its operations and crime statistics in the Press, particularly in view of the adverse publicity garnered by their controversial activities during the G20 protests and the furore surrounding the tragic death of newspaper seller Ian Tomlinson who was held to have been unlawfully killed[22] after he was pushed to the ground by a police officer.

However, there are more overt links between the Met and the Press and these ties ultimately led to the resignation of Met Police Commissioner Sir Paul Stephenson. Sir Paul had hired former *NOTW* Executive Editor Neill Wallis as a PR advisor to the Met, while Wallis was simultaneously in the employ of News International and was allegedly feeding them crime based stories for publication[23]. When Wallis was arrested as part of *Operation Weeting* details regarding this apparent conflict of interest found their way into the public domain. Although the Met Commissioner denied any knowledge of Wallis' links to phone hacking he nevertheless decided to resign in an effort to limit the damage being caused to Scotland Yard's reputation by his association with the scandal.

An additional strand of the hacking story is the existence of extremely close ties between the ruling political establishment and the media in Britain and the extent to which the powerful position of the media may have sheltered them from being subjected to appropriate scrutiny.

Traditionally politicians have courted the media in an attempt to win votes or garner public support for policies and reforms. Winston Churchill notably enjoyed close relationships with a number of the newspapers barons of the day including Lord Beaverbrook, while Margaret Thatcher benefited from the unwavering support of Rupert Murdoch throughout her three terms in office – even in respect of some of her most unpopular policies. In the modern media age these ties are arguably more important than ever.

The media's power to influence politics is probably best exemplified by the blistering attack launched by the Murdoch owned paper *The Sun* on Labour Leader

22   http://www.tomlinsoninquest.org.uk/tomlinson/
23   http://www.guardian.co.uk/uk/2011/sep/23/news-world-paid-wallis-met

Neil Kinnock on the day of the 1992 General Election when the headline on the front page of the paper proclaimed *"If Kinnock wins today will the last person to leave Britain please turn out the lights"*. When the Conservatives went on to win the election the tabloid proudly announced: *"It was The Sun wot won it"*. The redtop then backed Tony Blair's Labour Party before its landslide victory in 1997 before switching back to supporting the Tories just in advance of their narrow win in the General Election of 2010, indicating that the media has tended to take a mercenary rather than an ideological approach to party politics. The media and Rupert Murdoch in particular have frequently positioned themselves as political kingmakers. However, this is a very risky game for both sides to play, as just as you cannot be all things to all men, you cannot keep all newspapers happy at all times, particularly in today's competitive environment.

Chapter 7

The press on trial

"Remorse is the echo of a lost virtue"

(Edward G Bulwer-Lytton)

Notwithstanding the dearth of related press reports, arguably a symptom of the closing of ranks among many newspapers, it was becoming patently clear that the initial investigations into the early vestiges of the phone hacking scandal were by no means probing or exhaustive. The more information that surfaced about the depths that some of the tabloids had gone to in their attempts to source even more salacious material, the more apparent it became that the situation required a root and branch investigation. Clearly the *News of the World* was going to have to do much more in facing up to the misdemeanours of its employees if News Corporation were to have any chance of undoing the damage inflicted on its corporate integrity.

The Metropolitan Police came under a concentrated attack from those sections of the media which had chosen to buck the trend and even write about the scandal. However, such was the public outrage that even the tabloids were left with no alternative but to at least show some degree of concern and regret. Behind the scenes there was a clear inference that the widespread failure to focus on the real culprits was a direct result of the seemingly cosy relationship between the police, politicians and the press. That relationship was to be the subject of close examination which would in turn lead to the resignation of the Police Commissioner, Sir Paul Stephenson who, as mentioned earlier, stepped down having been the subject of serious criticism for his decision to employ Neil Wallis, a former executive editor of the *News of the World*, as a personal advisor to the Met in 2009.

As discussed in the previous chapter, the upshot of the renewed calls for a thorough, wide-ranging inquiry was the creation of a new police team which had been specifically set up to investigate the phone hacking affair. *Operation Weeting* was the immediate reaction to a national crisis, but if it had been introduced when these concerns first came to light, it may well have prevented the more serious excesses of a rampant press, or at least shone a light on the abhorrent lack of journalistic ethics at a time when much of the subsequent damage could have been prevented. *Operation Weeting* does not have defined terms of reference, but rather has been commissioned to find all and any evidence relevant to the inquiry.

In April, 2011, the *Operation Weeting* team made a number of arrests, including Neville Thurlbeck, chief reporter at the *News of the World* and Ian Edmondson, the former assistant news editor, both of whom denied any involvement in illegal activity. At around the same time, several sizeable damages payouts were made to phone hacking victims, including a payment of £100,000 to Sienna Miller[1], following complaints that her private phone messages had been intercepted. Other payments were made to Kelly Hoppen, Sienna Miller's stepmother and to politician Tessa Jowell and her husband David Mills. These payouts preceded an unprecedented apology from the *News of the World*. The language used in the apology makes much of the newspaper's award winning journalism in an attempt to remain staunchly proud in the face of public exposure of ever more cover ups surrounding the hacking scandal:

> *"Following an extensive internal investigation and disclosures through civil legal cases, News International has decided to approach some civil litigants with an unreserved apology and an admission of liability in cases meeting specific criteria.*
>
> *We have also asked our lawyers to establish a compensation scheme with a view to dealing with justifiable claims fairly and efficiently.*
>
> *This will begin the process of bringing these cases to a fair resolution with damages appropriate to the extent of the intrusion.*
>
> *We will, however, continue to contest cases that we believe are without merit or where we are not responsible.*
>
> *That said, past behaviour at the News of the World in relation to voicemail interception is a matter of genuine regret. It is now apparent that our previous inquiries failed to uncover important evidence and we acknowledge our actions then were not sufficiently robust.*
>
> *We continue to co-operate fully with the Metropolitan Police. It was our discovery and voluntary disclosure of this evidence in January that led to the re-opening of the police investigation.*
>
> *With that investigation on going, we cannot comment further until its completion.*
>
> *News International's commitment to our readers and pride in our award-winning journalism remains undiminished.*
>
> *We will continue to engage with and challenge those who attempt to restrict our industry's freedom to undertake responsible investigative reporting in the public interest."*[2]

Sienna Miller had been the victim of what can only be described as a campaign of press harassment in the months and years preceding her settlement with the newspaper. There were years when there was rarely a day that went by without the

---

1   See Statement in Open Court: http://www.atkinsthomson.com/07.06.2011%20-%20Sienna%20 Miller%20Statement%20in%20Open%20Court.pdf
2   See statement in full: http://www.bbc.co.uk/news/uk-13011504

publication of more photographs of the actress in some publication or another. The aggressive media attention that she was receiving became so intrusive that she was forced into the courts time and time again under the banner of several different causes of action[3] in order to take steps to protect herself.

One of the actress's first forays into the battle for privacy resulted in photographs being taken of her while she was filming *Hippie Hippie Shake* in 2007. During the course of filming the actors had filmed a scene in which they jumped into a lake naked. Sienna Miller was the target of the long lens photographer who, overcoming a high security presence, managed to take a series of naked photographs of her which were then sold to a photographic agency and subsequently published by the *News of the World* and the *Sun*. Miller sought and was awarded an injunction in respect of further publication of the photographs, arguing that the actions of the photographer, the photographic agency and News Group Newspapers, constituted a photographic invasion of her privacy. The case against the newspapers and the photograph agency settled for a record sum of £37,500 in damages. In January 2008, the Court awarded her default judgment and an injunction against the photographer who had employed surreptitious methods to get the photographs of her.[4]

Miller was again forced into fighting her privacy corner in September 2008 when the *Daily Star* infringed her right to privacy in publishing a photograph of her taken in Los Angeles. Her action against the newspaper settled for £15,000[5] and the terms included undertakings and an apology from the paper, which was forced to concede that Miller was "*extremely harassed and distressed by persistent pursuit and intimidating tactics*". Later that year, Miller invoked the Protection from Harassment legislation[6] in the first claim of its kind against a photographic agency. Needless to say, when she learned that, to cap it all off, the *News of the World* had been hacking her phone, she did not delay in seeking redress in the courts.

In the meantime, as the full extent of phone hacking scandal was about to be exposed and the *News of the World* was taking tentative steps to undo the harm that they had caused, behind the scenes the Metropolitan Police were still trawling through the tens of thousands of pieces of scrawled information that Glenn Mulcaire had left in his wake, which reportedly ran to some 11,000 pages containing 5,000 landline telephone numbers and 4,000 mobile phone numbers.

Among the ongoing challenges for the *Operation Weeting* team was the requirement to confront the indignation of many who believed that the scope of the investigation ought not to be restricted to the activities of Mulcaire but should also encompass the decidedly murky dealings of another private investigator, Jonathan Rees.

---

3   Miller has invoked Privacy law as well as protection from harassment legislation in order to counter press intrusion
4   *Sienna Miller v NGN Limited, Xposure Photo Agency Limited and Warren Richardson* Unreported. See Press report http://www.lawgazette.co.uk/gazette-in-practice/legal-updates/media-law-23
5   Out of Court settlement. See Press report http://news.bbc.co.uk/1/hi/entertainment/7644037.stm
6   Protection from Harassment Act 1997

Rees was no stranger to scandal and his movements have been the subject of close scrutiny ever since the brutal murder of his former business partner, Daniel Morgan, in 1987. Rees has been accused on numerous occasions of employing the questionable services of some less honourable members of the police force, who he seemingly relied on for information in the course of his private investigations. Furthermore, in 2000, Rees had been given a seven year custodial sentence, having been charged with attempting to pervert the course of justice as a result of planting cocaine on an innocent woman in a bid to undermine her credibility in a child custody battle. Upon Rees's release from prison it transpired that he was subsequently employed by Andy Coulson in his then capacity as editor of *News of the World*, prompting calls into not only Coulson's lack of judgment but also his personal and journalistic ethics.

The situation took a further dramatic twist when it was revealed that the *News of the World* had been hacking the phone of Milly Dowler[7] after she was abducted and alleged to have erased messages on her phone, giving false hope to her parents and adding confusion at a crucial stage of the police investigation. This was a different matter completely and something that the general public, and indeed the world at large, were not prepared to tolerate under any circumstances.

The tabloid's problems were further compounded when, within a matter of days, it was reported that *News of the World* journalists were also hacking into the phones of relatives of service personnel killed or injured in Afghanistan and Iraq[8]. Not only did this revelation embarrass and humiliate News Corporation, but it also undermined the credibility of the PCC and the Government, with the Prime Minister immediately being put on the back foot as a result of what appeared to be an all too snug relationship with the Murdoch family and their editor in chief, Rebekah Brooks, not to mention his decision in appointing former *NOTW* editor, Andy Coulson, as his PR chief. Although the Prime Minister had acted quickly in attempting to distance himself from not only News Corporation, but the press generally, it appeared to be too little and too late. In just one month, the unacceptable conduct of one section of the national press had brought to light the cosy dealings between the press and politicians, the apparent lack of regulation of the newspaper industry, and the lengths that certain elements of the media were prepared to go to in order to get an exclusive.

The information leaks that would herald the exposure of the Milly Dowler scandal would become the subject of a further tranche of litigation when the *Guardian* reporters who had learned of the gross infringement of the family's privacy, refused to hand over information relating to their police sources to the Metropolitan Police. The Met's objectives were to uncover the source of the leak within the police as

7   Revealed by *The Guardian* on 4 July 2011, http://www.guardian.co.uk/uk/2011/jul/04/milly-dowler-voicemail-hacked-news-of-world
8   Again revealed by *The Guardian* on 6 July 2011, http://www.guardian.co.uk/media/2011/jul/06/news-world investigator-families-dead-soldiers

part of their investigations into corrupt police officers and their links with the *News of the World*. They threatened *The Guardian* with the Official Secrets Act legislation[9] in a bid to force them to hand over the contentious information. The press argued that it was their unimpeachable right not to be forced to reveal their journalistic sources. As part of its investigation, the Met arrested *The Guardian* journalist, Amelia Hill and questioned her in relation to the passing of information from police sources to the newspaper. Her arrest was widely criticised by the press and by a number of politicians, one of whom, Tom Watson MP, proclaimed that:

> *"It is an outrageous abuse and completely unacceptable that, having failed to investigate serious wrongdoing at the News of the World for more than a decade, the police should now be trying to move against The Guardian which exposed this scandal."*[10]

The Met were in no doubt as to who should remain the focus of their investigations. The clamour for protection to be afforded to the concealment of journalistic sources proved to be overwhelming and the action was subsequently dropped.

The phone hacking scandal was at its zenith when the public announcement was made that Rupert Murdoch, moving decisively, had ordered the immediate closure of that great bastion of tabloid journalism, the *News of the World*, and the suspension of key players in his corporate structure. This was a clear indication of how seriously Murdoch was treating the problem, and the extent of the perversion of journalistic standards within the group.

The final edition of the tabloid was published on 10 July 2011, with the paper admitting *"We lost our way"*[11]. The decision had reportedly been accelerated by the threatened mass boycott of advertisers in the days and weeks leading up to the announcement. Among those who pulled their advertisements from the newspaper were the Co-Operative Group and General Motor Company. Numerous other companies hinted at their intention to cease to advertise with the organisation in response to the scandal.

Almost simultaneously, on 8 July, Andy Coulson was arrested on charges of phone hacking and making illegal payments to police, in the culmination of a reinvigorated enquiry by Scotland Yard. Assistant Commissioner John Yates expressed extreme regret that this action was not taken sooner, with reference to the discontinuance of the previous investigation which had led to the prosecution of Glenn Mulcaire and *News of the World's* former royal editor, Clive Goodman – ultimately leading to the pair being jailed in January 2007.

The scandal extended to the entire News International group, when the *Sunday Times* became immersed in allegations that it had behaved in an unethical and underhand manner in obtaining personal information belonging to former

---

9   Official Secrets Act 1989

10   http://www.telegraph.co.uk/news/uknews/phone-hacking/8770084/Phone-hacking-Guardian-journalists-told-to-reveal-Milly-Dowler-hacking-source.html

11   http://www.guardian.co.uk/media/2011/jul/09/news-of-the-world-thank-you-and-goodbye

Chancellor of the Exchequer, Gordon Brown. Another Group tabloid, the *Sun* was implicated when it was accused of similar misdeeds in relation to private medical records belonging to Brown's son, Fraser. The range and depth of the problem within News International was such that within a few weeks the Group was forced to withdraw its bid for full ownership of the global media company, BSkyB. This represented the most profound long term impact for the company and its shareholders from the scandal which elements of its media business had become embroiled in over the course of the spring and early summer.

On 15 July, Rebekah Brooks resigned as Chief Executive, albeit on conciliatory terms, having come under intense pressure from politicians and the public to step down from her role. In her retirement announcement she stated *"As Chief Executive of the company, I feel a deep sense of responsibility for the people we have hurt and I want to reiterate how sorry I am for what we now know to have taken place. At News International we pride ourselves on setting the news agenda for the right reasons. Today we are leading the news for the wrong ones"*[12]. Her decision was endorsed by both sides of the political divide, with David Cameron's spokesman agreeing that *"it was the right decision."* The leader of the opposition, Ed Miliband had been calling for her resignation for ten days in the run up to her final departure. Two days after her resignation, however, she was arrested on suspicion of conspiring to intercept communications and on suspicion of corruption. At the same time, the controversy regarding Metropolitan Police Commissioner, Sir Paul Stephenson's links to former *News of the World* deputy editor, Neil Wallis, came to light, leading to the resignation of London's top police officer.

The scandal had gone beyond the walls of News International, as the Assistant Commissioner of the Met, John Yates also resigned following revelations that he had helped secure a civilian role in the Metropolitan Police for Amy Wallis, daughter of the now ubiquitous Neil.

A further, entirely unexpected drama followed with the unexplained death of one of the *News of the World's* primary whistleblowers, Sean Hoare. Hoare's body was discovered at his North London home on 18 July 2011 and the news sent ripples of shock throughout the media world. Hoare had been in journalism since the 1980s, having worked as a trainee reporter on the *Watford Herald* and finding his way into the entertainment and showbiz columns at the *News of the World.* Hoare would reminisce fondly of the days when he would party with the stars, in a world fuelled by drink and drugs, the toxic combination that has been unofficially linked to his death.

Hoare had made a fundamental contribution to the investigations on phone hacking, perhaps the most important being his complete rebuttal of Andy Coulson's denials. Hoare is reputed to have said that it was common practice for journalists to be asked to perform their "dark arts"[13] on stories and it was widely known and understood that the subtle suggestion was in fact a command to go and hack

---

12   Rebekah Brooks Resignation Letter http://www.guardian.co.uk/media/2011/jul/15/rebekah-brooks-resignation-letter
13   http://www.guardian.co.uk/media/2010/sep/04/andy-coulson-phone-hacking

into someone's phone. Hoare's overview of the world of journalism in the heady years when the *News of the World* purported to be at the top of its game, gave an invaluable insight into this seemingly out of control arena.

On 19 July 2011, Rupert and James Murdoch appeared before the House of Commons Culture, Media and Sport Select Committee, with Mr Murdoch Senior advising the MPs that he was not aware of the extent of the phone hacking and that he had been let down by people he trusted. Mr Murdoch managed to leave the Select Committee hearing relatively unscathed by the questioning from the MPs.

However, this may not be the end of the matter so far as the Parliamentary Committee is concerned – certainly for James Murdoch whose performance was deemed to have been much less authoritative and convincing than that of his father. In the days following their appearance before the Committee, two former *News of the World* executives came forward to publicly accuse Murdoch Jnr of misleading MP's in his evidence. They questioned his claim that he was unaware of an email[14], the contents of which proved that more than one "rogue" reporter had been involved in phone hacking, and insisted that they had informed him of the contents before securing his agreement to settle the Gordon Taylor case.

When it was beginning to look like things could not possibly get any worse for News Corporation, they did, with it being reported on 28 July that Sara Payne, the mother of an 8 year old girl who had been murdered by a paedophile in 2000, had also been the victim of phone hacking. The news was almost beyond the comprehension of observers and the public alike given the close ties between Mrs Payne and those at News International who had helped publicise her long battle to have the names and addresses of paedophiles made public – better known as "*Sarah's Law*". It was her friends at *The Sun*, Rebekah Brooks the most notable amongst them, who helped Payne's personal battle for justice remain in the headlines and who were responsible for garnering the enormous level of public support for her campaign. So convinced was Mrs Payne of the worthiness of the newspaper that only weeks previously she had written a column in the last edition of the News of the World, saying that the staff at the paper had, "*supported [her] through some of the darkest, most difficult times of [her] life and became [her] trusted friends*"[15].

In the meantime, the controversy surrounding the appointment, the subsequent resignation and arrest of Andy Coulson had brought into sharp focus the nature of links between politicians and the press in British society. Indeed, David Cameron was forced to publish details of meetings with members of News International, including dates when Rebekah Brooks and Andy Coulson were his guests at Chequers. However, these close ties to the press are not unique to the Conservative Party; indeed Labour Prime Minister Gordon Brown had invited Brooks to Chequers and reportedly he and his wife had attended her wedding. There is evidently an

---

14   The so-called "for Neville" email named for its connection to *NOTW* reporter Neville Thurlbeck
15   http://www.newstatesman.com/blogs/the-staggers/2011/07/phone-given-sarah-payne-brooks

inherent danger in the extremely close relationship politicians have with the Press generally, with each needing the other's goodwill at different times and in different ways, which in turn leads to persistent, and often inappropriate, mutual "back scratching". The influence and power of the Press in the modern age means this relationship is inevitable. In the past newspapers have demonstrated their ability to affect public opinion and even impact election results, such as the example relating to the *Sun's* attack on Neil Kinnock on the morning of the 1992 General Election mentioned in Chapter 6.

Furthermore, the general public is kept very much in the dark as to the extent of this mutual co-operation and support, which although more blatant in the United States is, as recent events have revealed, quite a strong phenomenon in the UK too. Perhaps some good will come out of the phone hacking scandal if it serves to highlight this totally inappropriate relationship and the inability of the press to regulate themselves through the PCC. The big question is whether our elected members of Parliament who are so dependent on the press for their public standing, particularly in the run up to a general election, will be prepared to introduce legislation giving a suitably independent regulator strong and effective regulatory powers.

There are perhaps some grounds for optimism. After coming under considerable public and political pressure David Cameron announced that he would be establishing a judge-led Public Inquiry into the hacking scandal, headed by Lord Justice Leveson assisted by a panel of independent experts including a number of broadsheet editors and human rights experts. The Inquiry's terms of reference were to investigate culture, practices and ethics of the press in connection with its relationships with the public, the police and politicians. Preliminary hearings began in September 2011 with a number of high profile hacking victims being awarded "core participant", status including Kate and Gerry McCann, Max Mosley and Hugh Grant.

The Leveson Inquiry team, and in particular Lord Justice Leveson himself, had to deal with a number of preliminary wrangles before getting to the real heart of the matter. In late September, he was confronted by a conglomerate of media organisations which expressed concerns that the tabloid press was not effectively represented in his panel of advisors, and indeed that those advisors lacked experience in the sphere and genre of tabloid journalism. His panel line-up, as appointed by the Prime Minister, comprised Shami Chakrabati, director of Liberty; Sir David Bell, former chairman of the Financial Times; Lord David Currie, the former chairman of Ofcom; George Jones, former political editor of the Daily Telegraph; Sir Paul Scott-Lee, former chief constable of West Midlands police and Elinor Goodman, the former political editor of Channel 4 News.

Put very succinctly by Gillian Phillips, Director of Editorial Legal Services at Guardian News and Media, the main thrust of the complaints concerning the panel was that, *"tabloid and mid-market papers, as well as regional papers, will play a vital part in the story and we believe it is important that those assisting the inquiry reflect the plurality and divergence of the wider UK media."*[16] The concerned members of the media felt

16   http://www.pressgazette.co.uk/story.asp?storycode=47956

that Lord Justice Leveson's rather highbrow panel would not have the requisite understanding of this medium of the masses to deliver fair and just advice to their Chair. Whilst conceding that he had a "vast and difficult task" before him, Leveson countered that he was there to represent the views of everyone and would deliver his report on that basis, notwithstanding the significant differences in the stances of the various parties involved in his terms of reference.

Accordingly, it was quite apparent, notwithstanding the outrageous abuse of power by significant sections of the tabloid media, that we still had a situation where their "peers" felt comfortable enough to demand they be properly represented in a position of influence on the Leveson inquiry. Given that the press had already been given total free rein in their appointments to the PCC, and given its obvious failings, it is quite surprising that the press representatives even had the audacity to put forward such a proposal against such a controversial background.

However, the tabloids, despite their recent behaviour, are arguably a fundamental element in any democracy. Perhaps even their most robust critics would have to concede that it is the job of the tabloids to report on matters of public importance. The skill of the good tabloid reporter, to be capable of interpreting complex issues of public life and expressing them in accessible terms, is a vital one that clearly needs to be cultivated and encouraged. While it is justifiable to lament the lack of editorial control or any sort of moral compass displayed by some tabloid newspapers, they do still have an important role in informing people about matters that impact upon their daily lives. This should be their concentration rather than debasing themselves in their constant pursuit of higher sales through the presentation of more and more salacious material, which does nothing to keep their readers up to date with more important current affairs. What is apparent to almost all commentators is the fact that the tabloids have lost their way and need to critically reassess their overarching objectives in order to try and find it again.

September 2011 certainly saw a high degree of speculation and analysis in relation to the issue of privacy and the rights of the individual to protect him or herself from infringement. A high profile reminder of the harm that can be occasioned as a result of illegal infringement came at the expense of the US actress, Scarlett Johansson, who was the victim of a hacker's successful attempt to pry into the data that she held on her mobile telephone. Upon accessing her photographs, the hacker proceeded to leak them to various online celebrity sites, much to the consternation of Johansson and her legal team.

"Cease and desist" letters were swiftly despatched to a number of websites from Johansson's California-based lawyer, Marty Singer, advising that they "govern themselves accordingly" and that any failure to do so would be "at their own peril". It later transpired that his client was not the only celebrity to have had to endure the violation of their privacy in this manner, and that there were some 50 female stars whose telephones had been similarly hacked. The California Police undertook an investigation in order to get to the bottom of the illegal activities which were reported to have been perpetrated, not by an individual, but rather by a group of hackers, all primarily motivated by the unlikely thrill of causing shock, outrage and a not inconsiderable degree of titillation through their devious interference.

Also, on an international note, the phone hacking scandal has brought to light the similarities of the relationships between politicians and the press on both sides of the Atlantic, with both the US and the UK political establishments seemingly keen to not only curry favour with the press, but also to ensure that certain favoured elements of the media are kept close, tending to become more confidants rather than conduits of the powers that be. The speed with which the libel tourism legislation hurtled through the US Senate, with such a priority and with administrative corners being cut on an unprecedented basis, was a clear illustration of the power of the press in controlling not just the politicians, but also key legislation.

Certainly it is most unlikely that the SPEECH Act would have come about if it were not for unrelenting pressure from the US Publishers Associations, in the same way that the reform of UK libel legislation would not have attracted such intense parliamentary scrutiny in the absence of the intense pressure from the publishing industry in the UK.

Chapter 8

Access to justice

"There is far too much law for those who can afford it and far too little for those who cannot".

(Derek Bok – American educator and lawyer)

What are the remedies available to the victim of a defamatory publication? Obviously litigation, or the threat to litigate, would be the first option to be considered by a wronged individual following on from the immediate trauma of reading a dramatic headline article. On the other side of the coin, this is precisely what a publisher will want to avoid, or at least the financial costs of doing battle in the Courts.

The general perception of media lawyers is that we are an avaricious bunch determined to profit from the misfortune of our clients to such an extent that we cannot wait to issue proceedings and jump aboard what is generally perceived to be a limitless money train. However, unlike many other forms of litigation, libel proceedings are extremely unpredictable and, unless the client is very wealthy, the lawyer is effectively himself left to make most of the core decisions on the basis of minimising the financial risk to the client, or at least give carefully considered advice in light of the risks, which will dictate whether or not the client proceeds with a full blown action. Indeed, in many cases, particularly those involving contingency fee arrangements, it is the lawyer who will be under the most intense pressure to achieve a result sooner rather than later, while he looks over his shoulder at the dramatically escalating costs being incurred on the defence side, never mind his client's exposure to his own fees. The client will be very dependent on the advice and guidance of his lawyers as to his potential financial exposure in what are usually extremely unpredictable and ever changing circumstances. For instance, while a robust response is normally a fairly predictable reaction from most newspaper editors or legal departments, much less certain is whether they will decide to test the general resolve of the Claimant by engaging in the litigation process, with all the incumbent financial risks for both sides.

In all of these cases, decisions have to be taken quickly, with the financial consequences unravelling at each twist and turn. This is often an extremely intimidating experience for a Claimant, even the most seasoned of campaigners, given that many of these cases are dragged into the media spotlight from an early stage, with all the additional pressure that this involves. As has been stated on many occasions, *the libel Courts are not for widows and orphans.*

Libel litigation is certainly not for the faint hearted. While the "rich and famous" are often cited in the press as being the main beneficiaries of our legal system and may not be troubled by the same financial concerns as the rest of us, nonetheless they too will be taking a significant risk in terms of reputational damage in the event that the Court is not satisfied or convinced by their arguments. The description "libel lottery" is often not that far off the mark, at least in the early stages of litigation.

A client will normally be on the phone within moments of reading a derogatory article in the mistaken belief that just because the allegation is untrue, or does not meet with his approval, a newspaper will simply roll over and apologise in their next edition. This simply does not happen. Most broadsheets do take a responsible approach to publication, or at the very least will check their facts carefully and make a calculated assessment as to whether they can stand over their allegations on the basis of the evidence they have managed to gather. However, in the case of many tabloids, the only question is whether they can simply "get away with it." Both scenarios add up to the same predicament for the victim. With no option for an immediate resolution, he has to decide whether to take his chances with the consequent financial exposure, even when the case appears to all intents and purposes to be a "penalty kick", or whether he looks for other options which tend, unfortunately, to be very thin on the ground.

Aside from financial considerations, a libel Action also involves a significant time investment on the part of the Claimant, which is frustrating both for the individual and his lawyers. A Claimant will typically have to wait for at least 12 months, and in some cases several years, before a case even reaches the door of the Court. This is an extremely long time to wait for the opportunity to vindicate your reputation, particularly when in this intervening period damaging allegations remain uncorrected and often continue to be disseminated extensively online.

The newspaper industry will always highlight the right of reply option, which can be in the form of a favourable article setting out the victim's point of view or a letter to the editor. However, the reality is that the press tends to be somewhat selective in what they will publish and certain sections will not countenance anything that would be critical or undermining of press freedom and their point of view.

Both the UK and Irish Governments have recently been exploring ways of reducing what are perceived to be the excessive costs of libel litigation. The Irish legislators have provided for a fast track procedure in the Defamation Act 2009[1], although this is only available to those claimants who are prepared to cede any claim they may have for financial compensation. The process has not been utilised as much as had originally been anticipated, perhaps because the view is that it still brings with it all the previous uncertainties and hazards for a Claimant, without the threat of a substantial damages award which would normally encourage a Defendant to be more amenable towards a negotiated settlement. In the UK, the Ministry of Justice has also been looking at this option, along with the possibility of a Small Claims Court model, but again the absence of damages as a "negotiating factor"

1   Defamation Act 2009 (http://www.irishstatutebook.ie/2009/en/act/pub/0031/)

removes one of the core leverage options for an individual taking on an often unrepentant newspaper defendant, leaving the claimant more likely to have to expose themselves to the risks of a full hearing.

In the UK the first obvious alternative to litigation would have been the PCC, but even before the recent controversies, this was widely regarded as a "toothless"[2] body, and suffering from a clear lack of independence and impartiality.

To be fair to the media, they are entitled to respond to this criticism of their regulating body by pointing out that we lawyers are regulated by the Law Society, a body also made up of and governed by our own number. However, the reality is that the PCC has been given every opportunity to establish that it is prepared to act with robust impartiality and to provide an effective remedy, but so far, as the public's perception is concerned, it has failed, particularly certain sectors of Irish society, albeit including several representatives of the newspaper industry.

Another alternative, which is beginning to gather momentum, is the option of mediation or some form of independent arbitration. The Pre-Action Protocol for Defamation in England and Wales requires parties to consider whether some form of alternative dispute resolution procedure would be more suitable than litigation. Parties may be required by the Court to provide evidence that alternative means of resolving their dispute were considered, and the Court may have regard to such conduct when determining costs.

A number of other jurisdictions impose compulsory mediation requirements on parties. California, for instance, has enacted legislation[3] encouraging the parties to most civil proceedings, to attempt to mediate before commencing litigation. This in turn still provides significant work and opportunities for those on the periphery of the legal profession to provide the necessary backup services to facilitate what is a significantly high volume of mediation requirements. Texas also operates a similar system and other States are gradually following suit. Mediation offers not only a much less costly road to achieving a satisfactory resolution for both parties, but it can also be implemented at an early stage, which in turn will provide, in the case of defamation, the possibility of immediate vindication, particularly in circumstances where the Claimant is primarily seeking a retraction and apology as opposed to substantial damages. He also has the option of retaining his own legal team to represent him at the mediation to ensure that his interests are protected at all times.

Both the Courts and influential Parliamentary Committees have recently been advocating mediation as an alternative to litigation, not only in terms of defamation suits, but also for matrimonial and commercial proceedings. Certainly the option of mediation would appear to be a very welcome alternative for the less financially well off, who at least would have an opportunity to have their grievance heard and at the same time be able to hear what evidence, if any, the newspaper has

2   Report of the Culture, Media and Sport Select Committee on Press Standards, Privacy and Libel (February 2010), para 531
3   California Evidence Code Section 703.5 and Sections 1115–1128

against them. The problem is that, ironically, the press and their lawyers have been extremely slow to embrace this option, which is strange given their vocal criticisms of what they perceive to be excessive legal costs. Accordingly, unless either judicial or statutory pressure is brought to bear on the parties, the individual judges viewing cases in their early stages can only use what is extremely limited influence to encourage the parties to participate in some form of alternative dispute resolution.

The House of Commons Joint Committee on the Draft Defamation Bill has suggested that any refusal to engage in mediation could be overcome by empowering Courts to impose "*significant cost penalties*"[4] on any party that fails to comply with the provisions of the Pre Action Protocol.

In their Report, the Joint Committee recommended that "*early neutral evaluation*"[5] should take place following the initial exchange of letters between parties, with the possibility of punitive sanctions for those who fail to "*constructively*"[6] engage with the process. The report further recommended that parties should consider the possibility of "*voluntary independent arbitration*", in respect of more contentious cases where mediation may not be appropriate. Both of these recommendations have the potential for becoming viable and cost effective alternatives to litigation.

European jurisdictions are also beginning to warm to the idea of mediation, having been encouraged by the apparent success of the Californian model. However, the recent introduction of mandatory mediation in Italian civil cases has proven extremely controversial, with lawyers threatening to go on strike at what they regarded as a draconian initiative by the Berlusconi Government.

In 2011 the former legal manager of Times Newspapers Ltd, Alastair Brett, together with Sir Charles Gray QC, established the *Early Resolution Scheme* for libel actions. The motivation behind this scheme is the simple but fundamental principle that every individual should have access to justice regardless of their financial status. *Early Resolution* offers parties a viable alternative to the financial risks which are inherent in High Court litigation. *ER* membership is open to anyone who produces material which could potentially be the subject of a defamation action, for example journalists, publishers, academics or broadcasters. Law firms who specialise in defamation law may also apply to become associate members of the *ER* scheme.

Under the scheme parties must voluntarily enter into an arbitration agreement, and an arbitrator will be chosen from a panel of experts. The *ER* scheme offers assistance with the drafting of the arbitration agreement and the selection of the arbitrator. The arbitrator, assisted by a panel of two lay assessors will decide meaning and other key issues which arise between the parties. Communications between the parties and the panel are entirely confidential and made on a without prejudice basis. Although the scheme is voluntary, any rulings handed down by the arbitrator or panel are binding on parties and cannot be appealed. Efficiency and cost

---

4   Joint Committee on the Draft Defamation Bill, *First Report* (2011) para 81 *http://www.publications. parliament.uk/pa/jt201012/jtselect/jtdefam/203/20302.htm*
5   Ibid, para.82
6   Ibid

effectiveness are paramount in the process and while parties are entitled to make written submissions it is envisaged that key issues should be resolved within 28 days of the appointment of the arbitrator. In addition, according to the founding principles of the scheme, commercial defendants who agree to participate will be expected to pay the initial cost of determining key issues.

While litigation is often described as an avenue of last resort, at present there are limited alternative options available to someone who has been the victim of a defamatory attack. Accordingly, unless and until we have some form of statutory intervention, the options for voluntary mediation are likely to be extremely limited. Judges are currently only in a position to suggest this form of alternative dispute resolution to the parties, but having no legal basis to enforce compliance, unlike their American counterparts, there is little realistic incentive for mediation.

We have read much in the press in recent times on the theme that our libel laws are being abused by the rich and famous, but there has been scant mention of the issue of access to justice for the ordinary man on the street. Libel Actions brought by well known individuals make the headlines, simply because the name of the Claimant alone will be enough to attract the reader's interest, giving the newspaper the double benefit of increasing sales, while still having the luxury of berating the unfairness of our libel laws unchallenged. It is probably fair to say that the press has no hesitation in reporting on the perceived antics of wealthy celebrities, but they do not like to be sued by them. This love-hate relationship has, of course, prevailed for many years, and in an obtuse way has suited both the press and the celebrity for their own particular purposes at different times. However, the reality is of course that both sides also treat this as a one way street, until one side or the other is deemed to have taken matters to excess. The international star has of course a very important advantage in that he or she will normally have the financial means to take on a wealthy tabloid and see their case through to the bitter end if necessary. However, this is not the case for the ordinary citizen who, in order to take on a media Defendant, will often have to be prepared to put their home on the line even to get their complaint close to the door of the Court, never mind a full blown Hearing.

The reason for this is that there is no legal aid available for defamation Actions and, thanks primarily to a very successful media campaign, there will no longer be automatic recovery of "after the event" insurance premiums. Perhaps of even more significance is the proposed reform of conditional fee arrangements (CFAs), whereby a solicitor agrees to take on a case on a "no win no fee" basis, but where the Defendant has to pay an enhanced fee in the event of a successful outcome. In some cases, this could be as much as a 100% mark up on ordinary fees. However, in his report on Civil Litigation Funding[7], Lord Jackson proposed sweeping reform of the current system. His principal recommendation was that CFA success fees and ATE premiums should no longer be recoverable from the other party and should instead be deducted from any damages awarded to the Claimant. He envisaged that this would be offset to a degree by a reciprocal 10% increase in the level

---

7   *Review of Civil Litigation Costs: Final Report* (December 2009) London: The Stationery Office

of general damages awarded to the Claimant. However, lawyers would only be permitted to recover a maximum of 25% of their client's damages by way of success fee. Given that the average damages award in a defamation Action remains relatively low, this proposal would appear to have little to recommend it.

While a mark up of 100% could certainly be regarded as excessive, other than in exceptional circumstances, the reforms outlined above would provide absolutely no incentive whatsoever to a solicitor to take on what is often extremely difficult and unpredictable litigation on a contingency basis, with all the risks and interim outlay involved. In this regard the abolition of CFA's and ATE insurance premiums is tantamount to "throwing the baby out with the bathwater". Surely other more measured reforms could be introduced in order to eliminate the risk of abuse whilst still preserving access to justice for those most in need. For example, strict eligibility criteria could be introduced to prevent corporations or wealthy claimants from taking advantage of these fee arrangements, and as the Bar Council have suggested, "*staged*"[8] success fees could be introduced in order to prevent 100% uplift being claimed in all but the most exceptional of cases.

The Joint Committee did react positively to the proposed "*Qualified One Way Costs Shifting*" protections in defamation actions. The "*QOCS*" scheme, as applicable to personal injury cases, ensures that a Claimant is not exposed to the risk of paying the Defendant's costs, unless he is deemed to have acted unreasonably or can afford to pay such costs. The decision to exclude defamation Claimants from the scope of this protection will inevitably have a negative impact on those who are financially less well off, thereby restricting access to the libel Courts for ordinary citizens.

Much of the clamour for reform has arisen out of *Campbell v MGN*[9] and MGN's subsequent successful appeal to the European Court of Human Rights[10]. This case arose after photographs of the model Naomi Campbell were published in the *Mirror* newspaper in 2001, showing her attending a drugs rehabilitation clinic. The photographs were accompanied by various allegations relating to her attempts to overcome a drugs habit, and generally lambasting the model, particularly after Campbell issued proceedings against the newspaper[11]. Given the sensitive nature of the photographs, she succeeded in an action for damages, effectively for violation of privacy (which was in law based on the tort of breach of confidence). In addition to damages, Campbell was also awarded her legal costs and her representatives duly presented MGN with a legal bill for £1,086,296.47. Out of this total amount, the sum of £594,470 had been charged for prosecuting the appeal of the case at the House of Lords, of which £279,981.35 comprised success fees under CFA.

---

8   Response of the General Council of the Bar's Law Reform Committee to the Joint Committee on the Draft Defamation Bill, (June 2011) para.76 http://www.barcouncil.org.uk/assets/documents/LRC%20Response%20Defamation%20Bill%20100611.pdf
9   [2004] UKHL 22
10   Case No 39401/04
11   One of the articles accused the model of "whinging about privacy" after which a small furore erupted on the pages of the tabloid about the expectations a celebrity should have as regards their being the subject of public intrigue

Indeed, the percentage uplifts over and above the base costs for solicitor's and counsel's fees were 95% and 100% respectively. After these costs were approved by the Court (in the process of taxation), MGN appealed Campbell's entitlement to recovery of costs at this level, particularly the success fees. Their motion eventually reached the House of Lords, where the newspaper argued that recovering success fees was not compatible with Article 10 of the European Convention on Human Rights. This is the provision that deals with freedom of expression as follows:

> *"Everyone has the right to freedom of expression. This right shall include freedom to hold opinions and to receive and impart information and ideas without interference by public authority and regardless of frontiers."*[12]

It could be said that there is an appreciable similarity to the First Amendment guarantee in this provision. However, this EC provision is crucially further qualified:

> *"The exercise of these freedoms, since it carries with it duties and responsibilities, may be subject to such formalities, conditions, restrictions or penalties as are prescribed by law and are necessary in a democratic society, in the interests of national security, territorial integrity or public safety, for the prevention of disorder or crime, for the protection of health or morals, for the protection of the reputation or rights of others, for preventing the disclosure of information received in confidence, or for maintaining the authority and impartiality of the judiciary."*[13]

This required the Court to carry out a balancing exercise in a similar fashion to the American Courts addressing the balance between the First Amendment and the individual's right to protect their reputation using the traditional, albeit heavily modified, defamation laws. As stated by the Court, the question was whether the imposition of success fees arising from CFAs, specifically in defamation actions, was such that it could be said to have interfered with the right of freedom of expression, upon which the media is obviously heavily dependent. If media defendants were going to face enormous success fees on any payment out of damages, there would be no encouragement to resolve cases. The newspaper would argue that this could have a "chilling" effect, or make the tabloids think twice, before publication of potentially defamatory material. Was this possibly a restriction on freedom to expression? This may be true if the definition of freedom of expression included the right to publish derogatory and invasive disclosures of personal information, or indeed crude allegations that were entirely false. Furthermore, there was the argument that the Plaintiffs in media cases tended to be celebrities or high ranking professionals or scientists or otherwise exceptionally well known individuals who would be unlikely to have difficulty funding such litigation. This had to be considered, however, in light of the overall aim of the CFA system. The nature of CFAs in the provision of enhanced access to justice for individuals, mostly of lesser means, aligned it with the individual's right to a fair trial as prescribed by Article 6

---

12 Convention for the Protection of Human Rights and Fundamental Freedoms Rome, 4.XI.1950 (European Convention on Human Rights), Article 10.
13 Ibid

of the Convention[14]. Accordingly, it was held that the system as a whole did not inherently interfere with freedom of expression; therefore there was no reason to disallow the success fees being paid over to Campbell's lawyers. The legislation[15] that established the system did not provide that a client engaging a solicitor under CFA had to be "enquired of as to their means", therefore the Court declined to address any apparent unfairness that may arise in an individual case where the claimant could have proceeded without a CFA, or in effect, did not have any need for it. The benefits of CFAs overall in terms of their permitting access to justice for the 'man on the street', outweighed any apparent unfairness that may have appeared to have arisen when the plaintiff was a person of means.

However, this was not the end of the cause from MGN's point of view, as after the original substantive verdict in the privacy case was delivered by the House of Lords, they had filed an application[16] in Strasbourg for the European Court of Human Rights to provide its adjudication on all of the issues, including the issue of costs. The European Court in turn devoted a significant part of its judgement to the issue of the disputed fees.

Early on in its decision, the Strasbourg Court pointed out that in accordance with section 12(4) of our own Human Rights Act 1998, which implements the Convention, a court *"must have particular regard to the importance of the right to freedom of expression and, where the proceedings relate to journalistic material... any relevant privacy code"*[17]. Somewhat ironically, the Court referred to Clause 3 of the PCC's *Code of Practice*, and held that those guidelines, in force at the relevant time, which had perhaps been somewhat overlooked, applied in relation to press freedom and privacy:

> *"i)   Everyone is entitled to respect for his or her private and family life, home, health and correspondence. A publication will be expected to justify intrusions into any individual's private life without consent.*
>
> *ii)   The use of long lens photography to take pictures of people in private places without their consent is unacceptable.*
>
> *Note – Private places are public or private property where there is a reasonable expectation of privacy."*[18]

In considering the matter of the compatibility of success fees with Article 10, the Court referred to the findings of the *Jackson Review*, as published in January 2010. In particular it focused on four flaws in the CFA regime as identified by Lord

---

14   Article 6(1) In the determination of his civil rights and obligations or of any criminal charge against him, everyone is entitled to a fair and public hearing within a reasonable time by an independent and impartial tribunal established by law. Judgement shall be pronounced publicly but the press and public may be excluded from all or part of the trial in the interest of morals, public order or national security in a democratic society, where the interests of juveniles or the protection of the private life of the parties so require, or the extent strictly necessary in the opinion of the court in special circumstances where publicity would prejudice the interests of justice
15   Conditional Fee Agreements Regulations 2000 (SI 2000/692)
16   On 18 October 2004
17   Human Rights Act 1998
18   Case No 39401/04, para 86

Jackson. In the first instance the report found that the regime allowed for anomalies where some parties, such as those involved in commercial litigation, could engage solicitors under CFAs with the consequence that success fees are then used as a "ransom" to force a defendant to settle. There was also a problem with insurer's actions against public bodies, where it would be the taxpayer that ultimately pays the inflated or "doubled" fees. The second issue raised was that, from a solicitor's point of view, while the CFA system had been established for the benefit of the client, the client in practice had no interest whatsoever in the level of fees (or success fees) that were run up on his bill of costs. Ultimately he would not pay any fees – if he lost he was not liable for costs, and if he won invariably costs were paid by the losing party. Therefore, there is little control over the costs incurred during an action, the taxation process only taking place after the event. The participating client practically speaking has no interest in how much he is charged.

Thirdly was cited the problem that the costs, with success fees added, that may accrue against an unsuccessful party can often be disproportionate to the liability involved in the case itself, which can make a mockery of the application of the scheme in lower value cases.

The final flaw was the sheer dissatisfaction that could be said to lie in the fact that it would be possible for some lawyers to "cherry pick" cases which had a higher prospect of success, so as to benefit from success fees on a consistent basis in order to increase profitability. This type of conduct was not outside the bounds of the CFA scheme, albeit that there was little evidence that this was actually common practice. However, the final consideration, to apply particularly to defamation actions, was that CFA funded libel actions had such a high success rate that the idea of any benefit accruing to the client of average means was completely undermined. The European Court, accepting these points, also in fact heard submissions from various third parties[19], such as NGOs concerned with their exposure to defamation actions.

Ultimately, in Campbell's case, the European Court of Human Rights found that the success fees implemented did constitute an interference with the Article 10 right of freedom to expression. While considering that the CFA scheme had the legitimate aim of broadly accommodating for the individual's right of access to justice, the ECtHR deferred to the numerous consultations and reviews, culminating in the Jackson Report, which had suggested that the CFA system was "fundamentally flawed". The Court concluded that the scheme exceeded the boundaries of proportionality allowed for an interference of Convention rights in pursuit of a legitimate aim, and highlighted this as being demonstrated particularly in the case before the Court.

This decision has been seized upon by the media to attempt to undermine the CFA system, with many calls for CFAs to be made unavailable to claimants in libel and defamation actions. However, it should be recognised that this was an

---

19   The Society Justice Initiative, Media Legal Defence Initiative, Index on Censorship, the English PEN, Global Witness and by Human Rights Watch at Case No 39401/04, paras 4, 184

exceptional case which was clearly distinguished by the Court and was by no means representative of the costs award in a typical defamation case.

In order to avoid a knee-jerk reaction in the wake of the ECHR's decision, it should be considered that, contrary to popular perception, CFA's are available to defendants as well as claimants and can also be used to in fact *protect* an individual's Article 10 rights and thereby *prevent* any "chilling" effect on free speech. One of the most well known examples of a defendant benefiting from the availability of a CFA is the case of Simon Singh, who used this arrangement to defend the lawsuit brought against him by the British Chiropractic Association (the "BCA"). Singh, the acclaimed scientist, author and columnist for *The Guardian* newspaper had, on 19 April 2008 published an article refuting claims allegedly made by the BCA that chiropractors were able to cure conditions other than back complaints, for example as asthma or colic in children, with the result that the article and Singh became the subject of a libel action taken by the BCA against the author directly. Taking his case to the Court of Appeal on the preliminary issue of whether the article should be construed as a statement of fact or opinion, Singh eventually won out on this skirmish in front of three Appeal Judges at the Royal Courts of Justice, who ruled that the statement had to be considered an opinion. This in turn entitled the author to use the defence of fair comment[20]. Subsequently, before the main action proceeded to trial, the BCA withdrew their proceedings[21].

The ability of an ordinary individual, as opposed to the celebrity or super-rich, to take on the might of the Press using a CFA is aptly demonstrated by the case involving Christopher Jefferies. Mr Jefferies was the landlord of Joanna Yates, who went missing from her Bristol apartment shortly before Christmas 2010 and was subsequently found murdered. Mr Jefferies would doubtlessly have been unable to counter the horrendous campaign of vilification carried out by the tabloid press without the aid of a CFA. Not only did Jefferies receive damages from eight newspapers that published articles implying that, based purely on his appearance and demeanour, he was Yeates's murderer, the Court also made rulings on the damaging effect that these stories could have had, had Mr Jefferies been required to defend himself in criminal proceedings[22]. Subsequently, the *Sun* and *Daily Mirror* tabloid newspapers were fined sums of £18,000 and £50,000 respectively for contempt of court[23]. Notwithstanding, despite grossly misleading headlines and lurid photographs of Mr Jefferies being published on the front pages of these newspapers, it was noted that printed apologies appeared only in small print on the second pages of the respective publications (following initial apologies read out in the High Court)[24]. It is little wonder that the family of Milly Dowler, who recovered damages from the *News of the World* on account of the hacking of her mobile phone, also with the aid of a CFA, had written directly to the Prime Minister

20   http://www.telegraph.co.uk/health/healthnews/7544666/Simon-Singh-wins-key-battle-in-alternative-medicine-libel-case.html
21   http://www.guardian.co.uk/science/2010/apr/15/simon-singh-libel-case-dropped
22   http://www.guardian.co.uk/media/greenslade/2011/jul/29/joanna-yeates-national-newspapers
23   http://www.guardian.co.uk/media/2011/jul/29/sun-daily-mirror-guilty-contempt
24   http://tabloid-watch.blogspot.com/2011/07/page-two-apologies-to-christopher.html

petitioning him not to press through reforms that proposed abolishing CFAs[25]. This entreaty to David Cameron, sent by the family on 19 September 2011, questioned, to paraphrase, whether the PM was *on the side of the people or the side of the press?*[26]

Other high profile beneficiaries of CFAs include the Tamil protestor Parameswaran Subramanyam[27], who would most likely have been left without any means of vindicating his reputation had such an arrangement not been available to him. In the future will individuals like this have no choice but to allow the media to destroy their reputations?

Furthermore, aside from any Article 8 or Article 10 considerations, there must be a potential breach of a Claimant's Article 6 right to a fair trial given that he is being deprived of access to justice in one of the most difficult areas of litigation, notwithstanding the attempts of a few personal litigants who have decided to take on the system.

There has been a general application of judicial consideration as to whether the right to seek financial assistance from the state (Legal Aid), will fall within the remit of Article 6 of the Convention. In the first instance, Article 6 does not contain a right to funding in civil cases but, demands that the Court make an assessment of a person's right of access to the court and right to a fair trial. The European Commission of Human Rights had dealt with the issue in the case of *W v UK*[28]. In this case the applicant had claimed that the absence of Legal Aid granted to plaintiffs to take defamation actions in the UK was a violation of Article 6 rights. This is relative to Legal Aid being more readily available for criminal and family cases, or certain other civil claims such as for compensation for personal injury. The ECHR held that it was not unreasonable to exclude certain categories of legal proceedings, including defamation, from public funding. In the case of *Munro v UK*[29], while the Commission accepted that the applicant was unable to afford legal representation, and that it would not be reasonable for them to appear as a personal litigant due to the complexity of the litigation, it nonetheless held that:

> "The general nature of a defamation action, being one protecting an individual's reputation, is clearly to be distinguished from an application for judicial separation, which regulates the legal relationship between two individuals and may have serious consequences for any children of the family. Defamation proceedings are moreover inherently risky and it is extremely difficult to accurately predict their outcome. The Commission recognises, furthermore, than the nature of a claim of defamation is such that it may be easily open to abuse..."[30]

A less tangible benefit arising from our current libel legislation is that readers tend to give much more credence to stories in the press in the knowledge that the

---

25   http://www.guardian.co.uk/uk/2011/sep/22/milly-dowler-cameron-legal-reform?newsfeed=true
26   http://www.guardian.co.uk/uk/interactive/2011/sep/22/dowler-family-letter-david-cameron
27   *Parameswaran Subramanyam v News Group Newspapers Ltd* (2010) Unreported
28   Application No 10871/84
29   Application No 10594/83, 14 July 1987, DR 52
30   Ibid

publisher has to give at least some credence to the requirements laid down by the law. The other side of the coin is of course that a Claimant's failure to sue would not necessarily be interpreted as an admission of guilt, as would currently be the case.

As discussed previously, if litigation is to be restricted to the wealthy elite, then significant reform will be necessary to strengthen other avenues of redress, including, inter alia, reform of the PCC, statutory intervention to encourage participation in ADR and clarification regarding the duty of the media to provide a right of reply and other appropriate remedies.

This choice is obviously one for the electorate and their political representatives to consider, but perhaps it is an equally relevant question for the media themselves, who have to decide whether it is appropriate for them to sacrifice the credibility and accuracy that is encouraged by our libel laws in return for what would be effectively an unfettered right to publish what they wanted with the minimum level of accountability. While the press may have jumped at such an opportunity several years ago, given the market erosion that the broadsheets in particular are experiencing due to the ever advancing reach of the online news websites, they may think twice before denouncing what is an important aura of credibility which may be one of its last lines of defence in protecting their current market share. Even the tabloids have to face up to the fact that they have serious competition from the online gossipmongers who are subject to virtually no regulations, but likewise are afforded little or no meaningful credibility while fighting for that crucial audience share.

The next few years will be a testing period for the media and the aforesaid decisions will undoubtedly have a crucial role in shaping the very future of the national press.

Chapter 9

The battle for privacy

"If privacy is outlawed, only outlaws will have privacy"

(Philip Zimmerman)

The power of the press when exercised responsibly represents a critical safety net for the basic freedoms in democratic society. However, as with all power, if it is not adequately harnessed and in the absence of any protection for those who are reliant on it, that power can be perverted to the point where it undermines the freedoms and values it is supposed to protect. While most broadsheet editors and mainstream publishers strive to exercise this power fairly and appropriately, they have come to see themselves as the final and only arbiter as to what is legitimate and reasonable. Their stance is all the more compromised due to the fact that nowadays speed often takes precedence over accuracy in a bid to win the race to publish the big stories. In many instances, editors display a basic reluctance to admit a wrong, particularly when publication has already taken place. This phenomenon applies equally to the laws of defamation and the rapidly developing battleground of privacy. While the press now believe that they have won the struggle for change in the law of libel, the emphasis is now shifting towards the even more sensitive issue of privacy.

Any reader of the tabloids, and indeed the broadsheets, would be forgiven for believing that the so called injustices emanating from our defamation laws were more newsworthy and important than say the civil chaos in the Middle East (and this was a common feature in the press on both sides of the Atlantic). Certainly the extent and intensity of the coverage must have taken the Manchester United and Wales football star Ryan Giggs[1], for one, by surprise. The high profile footballer had gone to considerable lengths to protect his privacy, and in particular his relationship with the former Miss World contestant Imogen Thomas by way of a super-injunction, but unfortunately this backfired in spectacular fashion when his legal cover was blown, not by the tabloids as would normally be the case, but on-line through that global phenomenon, *Twitter*. Suddenly it became open season on Giggs, as he came to epitomise the topic of the day in the media, the super-injunction, which in turn had completely the reverse effect in terms of protection. The case came as not just an unfortunate epitaph as his brilliant football career was coming towards its end, but also marked the likely swan song for this type

---

1   *CTB v News Group Newspapers Ltd* [2011] EWHC 1232 (QB)

of injunction, certainly so far as protecting the affairs of professional footballers is concerned.

Prior to the phone hacking scandal, two controversial matters had come to symbolise the often hysterical outcry surrounding the ever contentious issue of press freedom, namely the *Mosley*[2] case and the super-injunction. The "freedom of speech" issue was and remains a familiar feature in the defamation law debate, and this has now been transferred with seamless efficiency to the privacy controversy, with virtually the same arguments and complaints being transferred by the press to the arguments surrounding this issue.

The former head of Formula One motor racing, Max Mosley, brought a claim for breach of privacy against the *News of the World* after they had published footage of him allegedly engaged in masochistic games with a number of prostitutes in a basement cellar. One of the prostitutes had been fitted with a secret camera and the resultant footage was not only published extensively in the Sunday tabloid with various graphic allegations of Nazi role playing and other controversial conduct, but the entire footage was also broadcast to a worldwide audience on their website.

The newspaper editorial and legal teams no doubt took the view that they were totally safe from litigation in that they believed they had their victim caught bang to rights and that the sheer embarrassment alone would have deterred most people from even contemplating legal proceedings. However, Mosley proved to have a lot more resilience and sheer guts than they could possibly have anticipated, and went on to drag the *News of the World* through not only the UK but also the European Courts. In a landmark decision in the High Court in London, Mosley was awarded £60,000 for breach of his fundamental right to privacy (the cellar was deemed to be a private place). The Court held that there is a reasonable expectation of privacy in respect of sexual activity between consenting adults, and the *News of the World's* public interest defence was rejected on the basis that no crime had been committed and there was no evidence whatsoever to support the paper's allegations of a Nazi theme. Although significantly less than the six figure awards that are common in defamation actions, this judgment has set down a marker in terms of a "line in the sand", which, taken with the significant legal costs awarded against the newspaper, should cause the media to think twice before going to such lengths in the future.

Since that case, the emergence of the now seemingly widespread practice of phone hacking, featuring most prominently the *News of the World*, provided a further illustration of just how far the tabloid Press have been prepared to go in order to secure stories that will titillate their readers and, more importantly of course, increase the sales of their newspapers in what has become an extremely competitive business.

2   [2008] EWHC 687 (QB); (no 1 – 9 Apr 2008); [2008] EWHC 2341; (no 2 – 1 Jul 2008); [2008] EWHC 1777 (QB) (no 3 – 24 Jul 2008

The *News of the World*, even by its own acknowledgement, had sunk to new levels of depravity and press intrusion, when it was found to have hacked into phones belonging not just to celebrities, but also the mobile phone belonging to Millie Dowler as well as the phones of servicemen and their families. Indeed, the full extent of the phone hacking scandal may never be fully known but the statistics suggesting that more than 9,000[3] landline and mobile phones had been recorded in Mulcaire's notebooks says everything, and certainly puts into perspective media complaints regarding the "chilling effect" of our libel laws.

As alluded to earlier, lawyers need to be cautious when criticising the practice of self regulation, given that this applies equally to the legal profession, but the fact that a number of News Corporation employees have been members of the Press Complaints Commission, not to mention the editors of other publications, does call into question the decision by successive Governments to place their trust in the PCC, with or without the benefit of hindsight.

Phone hacking and secret filming – the words "Big Brother" come immediately to mind – and these are only the instances that we know about. Are these very personal intrusions limited to what the media like to classify as the "rich and famous"? What about the rest of us? Do we now have to exercise caution when gossiping with friends on our mobile phones or when enjoying that Saturday night chat over a bottle of wine? We have to remember that it is normally only cases involving controversial characters or sordid incidents that actually reach the Courts. These are the cases which the newspapers believe they have a good prospect of winning for the very reason that they are so embarrassing for the Claimant that it is hoped that they will either lose their nerve at the last minute or be unable to garner sympathy from a judge and jury. The publisher is therefore prepared to take a gamble, and as a result, we have the unusual situation that legal precedent is being established by "controversial" characters such as Max Mosley and Naomi Campbell. However, while their determination has won the day, their colourful history may explain why damages in privacy actions tend to be on the low side. This brings us back to the fundamental issue of deterrent.

Unlike defamation, where the general view, however questionable, is that a damaged reputation can be repaired by way of compensatory damages, once "the privacy horse has bolted" financial compensation is an inadequate and ineffective remedy. When private information or photographs have been published and, given the speed with which in the digital age, that this material is disseminated internationally, then the damage has not only been done, but is irreparable. Accordingly, it is absolutely vital in such cases that intrusive publication does not occur in the first place. Unfortunately, while damages in privacy cases remain at such a modest level, there is no real deterrent to discourage what are often blatant and provocative breaches of a person's, and indeed his or her immediate family's privacy, whether it be in the form of aerial photographs of the family home or salacious speculation as to sex life or personal habits.

3   Comments made by Deputy Assistant Commissioner of the Metropolitan Police Sue Akers. Reported: http://www.telegraph.co.uk/news/uknews/phone-hacking/8637940/Phone-hacking-police-contacting-30-victims-a-week.html

Max Mosley, who has become something of a privacy campaigner since his victory over the *News of the World,* applied to the European Court of Human Rights[4] on the basis that the UK owed a positive obligation under Article 8 to impose duty on the media to give prior notice of any invasion of privacy. His campaign for a *prior notification* requirement was premised on the fact that damages are an inadequate remedy to compensate an individual once private information relating to them has been placed in the public domain. This application was ultimately rejected by the ECtHR on the basis that a pre-notification requirement may have a *"chilling effect"* on the Press and given the wide margin of appreciation accorded to Member States by the Convention, Article 8 does not require the implementation of a legally binding pre-notification requirement.

A direct consequence of the absence of any financial deterrent has contributed to the rapid rise in the use of injunctive relief, and specifically, the super-injunction. The press really could not believe their luck when word started to come out that a number of well known professional footballers had taken out super-injunctions to prohibit reporting on their affairs. The hysteria that followed has added the expression "super-injunction" to the lexicon of words that will come to epitomise a social era in the years to come, and which has given the media more column inches than probably any other controversy in recent times. The very nature of a super-injunction, which prevents the press from reporting on the actual fact of the injunction and the identity of the individual taking it out as well as the subject matter, has in itself presented the press with an opportunity to not only distract the public's attention away from the phone hacking scandal but also to support their claim for dramatic changes in the attitude of the Courts to the protection of privacy, in tandem with changes to the libel laws which had previously been the main focus of the media. The issue has been further complicated by the fact that there is no law of privacy as such in the UK, but following the adoption of Article 8 of the European Convention on Human Rights, the Courts have been left with the unenviable task of attempting to interpret this Article on a case by case basis, while at the same time seeking to achieve a balance with the right to freedom of expression set out in Article 10.

Historically, in UK law there has never been a law of privacy as such and the only means of protecting the disclosure of private information has been through an Action in breach of confidence. However, law in this area has developed rapidly over the past decade and the catalyst for this development has been the incorporation of Article 8, which provides for the right to respect for private and family life into UK law following the enactment of the Human Rights Act 1998.

As a result of judicial interpretation of Article 8 in seminal cases such as *Douglas v Hello*[5], *Campbell v MGN*[6] and *Murray v Express Newspapers*[7], the law of privacy has gradually been developed. These decisions have been supplemented by

---

4   *Mosley v UK* no 48009/08 [2011] ECHR 774 (10 May 2011)
5   (No 3) [2006] QB 125
6   [2004] UKHL 22; [2004] 2 AC 457
7   [2008] EWCA Civ 446

ECtHR decisions, such as *Von Hannover v Germany*[8] where the European Court of Human Rights held that there is a positive obligation on Member States to protect privacy between individuals. However, Article 8 is not an absolute right and there is an inherent tension between this Article and the right to freedom of expression provided for by Article 10. The Convention was deliberately crafted in such a way as to require a delicate balancing act to be carried out between these two competing rights.

In re S (A child)[9], Lord Steyn stated that when the respective Articles are being balanced neither *"has as such precedence over the other"*.[10]

It is generally accepted that the Courts will apply a two stage test when deciding whether or not an individual's right to privacy has been breached, namely:

(i)   The Court must first determine whether there is a *"reasonable expectation of privacy"*, thereby engaging Article 8; and

(ii) If Article 8 is engaged, the Court moves on to balancing the competing Article 8 and Article 10 rights.

This brings us on to the question as to when there is a reasonable expectation of privacy? This is an objective test which will largely depend on the circumstances of each particular case including, inter alia, the attributes of the Claimant, the nature of the activity, the place where it was happening, the absence of consent, the extent to which the information was already in the public domain, the effect on the Claimant and the circumstances in which the information was obtained by the publisher. In *McKennit v Ash*[11], it was held that even trivial details can be afforded protection because of *"the traditional sanctity accorded to hearth and home"*[12].

At the second stage the Court will balance Article 8 and 10 interests, applying the test of proportionality. The Court will decide if the publication of the information pursues a legitimate aim and whether the benefits of doing so are proportionate to the harm which might be caused by interfering with the right to privacy. When conducting this balancing exercise, the Court will take into account the wider "public interest". In *Von Hannover*[13] this was expressed in terms of whether the disclosure contributed to a *"debate of general interest"* to society.

A further privacy case based on the European Court of Human Rights decision was delivered in the case of *Sciacca v Italy*[14]. The facts concerned a teacher in Sicily who had been put under house arrest during the course of a police investigation for tax evasion and the forgery of official documents. The police photograph that was taken as part of the investigation subsequently found its way into the press

---

8   (2005) 40 EHRR 1
9   (2005) 1 AC 593
10   Ibid, per Lord Steyn at para 17
11   [2006] EMLR 178
12   Ibid, per Eady J para 135
13   Von Hannover v Germany (see n8)
14   (2006) 43 EHRR 400

and despite her guilty plea in relation to the charges that were levelled at her, she successfully argued that the release of the photograph was a breach of her Article 8 rights.

It is interesting to note, in relation to the Court's reaffirmation of the principles in *Von Hannover*, that whilst the applicant in the *Sciacca* case had found herself the subject of a criminal investigation, she was not a 'public figure' for the purposes of the balancing act between privacy and freedom of speech, therefore meaning that the release of the photograph was an interference with her right to respect for her private life.

Although the approach by the Courts has been relatively consistent, the controversy surrounding super injunctions and the desire of the press for an unfettered right to publish whatever they deem appropriate has led to the inevitable conflict between Parliament and the Judiciary over the implementation of what can at best be described as legal uncertainty.

Over the years, the law itself has been developing to provide some degree of protection to the population at large, whether rich or famous or just someone struggling to make a living, with the deterrent of a financial penalty and the ultimate threat of a full blown Court hearing. As a result, the print media has, particularly in recent times, been focusing its considerable influence in attacking not only the law, but also the Courts and individual Judges. A classic example has been the persistent attacks on Mr Justice Eady, who, as previously mentioned[15], has been responsible for most of the recent key decisions in landmark defamation cases in the UK. Mr Justice Eady has subsequently been allocated fewer claims involving the media, with Mr Justice Tugendhat taking charge of the main case list. This marks a prime example of the power of the press and how that power can be corrosive of democratic principles rather than acting as the crucial "safety net" discussed at the outset of this chapter.

In any event, effective prevention rather than subsequent cure remains a fundamental problem in the laws of both defamation and privacy. While monetary compensation is all very well, often the victim will have to wait many months or years for vindication, throughout the process and even with a favourable outcome the victim will have to deal with the inevitable and often facile charge that there can never be "smoke without fire".

Another of the perils facing well known personalities is the risk that some warped individual, seeking fame or fortune (or indeed both), decides to fabricate an incident so as to embarrass or compromise the celebrity concerned. Often such allegations are of a sexual nature, ranging from an alleged sexual affair or inappropriate sexual conduct, usually taken to the extremes with a cry of rape or serious criminal offence. In such circumstances, the high profile individual is totally vulnerable to the whims and commercial motivation of the tabloid press, which is all too often more concerned with securing an "exclusive", rather than the feelings

15   See Chapter 4, page 60

or reputation of the celebrity, whose name and predicament will sell papers. The temptation to rush and get the "breaking news" often overrides the need to check the authenticity and accuracy of the story. It used to be the case that at least two independent sources were required to verify a story before it was allowed to go to print, but now that requirement is more often than not dispensed with, as the electronic revolution means the race to get the story out is at levels that are unprecedented and that no-one could have imagined ten years ago.

Unfortunately there is surprisingly little protection for the victim under not just UK law, but internationally, with the Dominique Strauss Khan case being a prime illustration of the catastrophic consequences of this phenomenon. One minute, Strauss Kahn is sitting in the first class cabin of an Air France flight about to enjoy the perks and privileges enjoyed by someone in his position on a long haul flight, when the next minute he was being paraded in front of the world's media in handcuffs, degraded and ostracised in a shorter time period than his flight could have made it across the Atlantic. This is in stark contrast to the significantly less dramatic and extensive media coverage surrounding the subsequent dismissal of all charges against him, after his accuser was found to have lied to police and prosecutors.

Without dwelling too long on the merits of this particular case, it clearly illustrates not only the catastrophic consequences for those in the limelight being wrongly accused, but also the sheer power and reach of the world's media, and the speed with which a story gets global attention and how with it a reputation – no matter how powerful the individual – can be damaged beyond repair.

Another recent example of this type of campaign is the case of Rebecca Leighton, a nurse at Stepping Hill hospital in Stockport, who was charged in connection with the contamination of saline bags which were linked to the deaths of five patients. The presumption of innocence was quickly abandoned as the tabloid press seized on this story, with sensationalist headlines proclaiming her guilt. Her privacy was also grossly violated by newspapers which hacked into her Facebook account and re-published photographs of her socialising as well as a photograph of her home. All charges against Ms Leighton were subsequently dropped; however, the damage caused to her reputation as a result of the reckless conduct of the media may be irreparable.

Unless you have been the victim of a personalised attack on your character by the media, it is very difficult to understand the daily torment that has to be endured before the record can be set straight and a reputation vindicated. Even if some warning is received, usually in the form of a series of questions forwarded within days, or often quite deliberately hours, before the publication deadline, nothing prepares you for the trauma of the bold headlines staring not just you in the face, but also the rest of the of the population. Although some people will have no hesitation in making their thoughts known to you, the vast majority will say nothing, with their silence being the most devastating indictment.

Accordingly, the only realistic preventative measure is an injunction ("super" or otherwise) which, if granted, restrains the newspaper from publishing the offending material in the first place, at least until a full Hearing can take place to determine the rights and wrongs of the situation. Indeed, the super-injunction has come to represent the struggle to balance the competing rights to a reputation in Article 8 and freedom of expression as provided for in Article 10.

However, the drafting by the European legislators of what was at the time a well meaning attempt to create some degree of uniformity in transnational law, has in effect probably introduced even more uncertainty and controversy than previously existed. This, in practice, has brought us no closer to producing a magic wand that could be used to determine when press freedom and the public interest takes precedence over the basic right to have our character and privacy protected against unfair criticism and intrusion.

The problem is exacerbated by the very fact that the prurient gossip and scandal that some of us enjoy from time to time, and thereby encourage the press to bring to us, by necessity involves intrusion into somebody's private life. While the public in general may have less sympathy for the straying footballer seeking to protect his sordid sex life, we do tend to be more sympathetic towards the infliction of unnecessary hurt on the victim's wife and children, when the story comes from within the four walls of a private home.

The question, therefore, that has to be asked, is who should decide what the public is entitled to know. The press will, of course, claim to be the bastion of freedom of expression and the protector of the public interest. However, it is increasingly self evident that this is not a credible position to argue. In circumstances where *self* interest is involved in the form of newspaper or book sales, how can they possibly act with appropriate impartiality, and if they get it wrong, what are the consequences, not so much for the publisher, but the victim?

Without seeking to be overly dramatic, perhaps a valid analogy is the sentencing of a convicted criminal to the death penalty. Apart from the moral arguments on both sides, the same consequences arise in that once the decision to execute has been carried out there is no return. The same principle applies to the publication of the vitriolic newspaper headline and article, which these days will travel around the world in seconds, and effectively becomes the point at which someone's reputation is killed by media execution with largely irreversible consequences for the victim. It would seem that without any prospect of a retrospective reprieve, and before the struggle between the basic freedoms can be determined, the rights of one side in the argument might as well not exist.

The problem here is that time is normally of the essence in investigative journalism. Both the broadsheets and the tabloids are in constant competition with their rivals to get their story out first, and there is always the risk that delay might compromise a source or allow a guilty culprit to cover his tracks, thereby prejudicing ongoing investigations. If the story was to be delayed, possibly for many months, as a result of injunctive intervention, this could possibly undermine and negate the often painstaking journalistic work that has gone into the investigation in the first place. Perhaps understandably, there is little incentive to give the victim advance notice of an intention to run a story, bringing us back to the fundamental issue of the deterrent.

The Americans adopt a fairly simplistic attitude to resolving this delicate balance of freedom by coming down firmly and almost exclusively in favour of freedom of speech. Under the First Amendment of the US Constitution, this freedom is afforded an overriding priority in virtually every conceivable circumstance, with the result that the US media can "publish" without fear of being "damned". Public figures are regarded, to all intents and purposes, as fair game, and the problem is that this classification extends far beyond the well-known politician or celebrity, and applies to virtually everyone holding public position, whether they are a police officer, a civil servant, or any other government official. The onus is very much on the subject to establish that what has been published is not only false but also that it has been published with malice – an often impossible task and one explanation as to why many Americans seek to avail themselves of the more claimant friendly UK legal system.

However unfair and one-sided the US approach may appear to be, it nonetheless does have the advantage of simplicity and clarity. Everyone knows where they stand and, while the price to be paid may be a media lacking the credibility afforded to the UK press, at least the victim will not necessarily be thought any less of by not taking the proactive step of seeking to vindicate his reputation through the Courts – as you really cannot believe everything you read in the American press.

Another option might be to extend the protection currently afforded to rape victims to include any individual who has been accused of an offence, meaning that their identity could not be revealed at least until they have been formally charged with a crime. While this would not have offered any protection to Strauss Kahn, it would have provided some degree of protection to the likes of entertainment promoter Louis Walsh, in dealing with what were the totally fabricated allegations being afforded front page headlines in *The Sun* newspaper before he had even been interviewed by the police. In June 2011, *The Sun* splashed pictures of Mr Walsh across its front page accompanied by the completely false and unfounded allegations. Although the source of these claims subsequently admitted that he had made the whole story up, serious damage had already been caused to Mr Walsh, with virtually every other newspaper picking up *The Sun's* story, resulting in worldwide coverage within a matter of hours of the initial publication. As the law currently stands, a celebrity victim is afforded absolutely no protection whatsoever from the devastating impact and consequences following on from such an outrageous publication.

In the meantime, the British press continues to adhere to its own version of "free speech". Although this may often be biased and lacking balance, nonetheless we are spared the more rampant excesses in the US media. That being said, and apart from the particularly disproportionate coverage of the libel and privacy debates, the UK and Irish press have always been regarded as being among the most credible in the world, probably in no small measure due to the sobering impact of our libel laws, which encourage greater caution and fairness in the editorial process.

Chapter 10

An international perspective

"Trying to determine what is going on in the world by reading newspapers is like trying to tell the time by watching the second hand of a clock."

(Ben Hecht)

Significant differences in the laws relating to privacy and libel exist not only between the US and the UK, but other European countries also have differing approaches, particularly in relation to the right to a private life. Some of these inconsistencies would appear to be more difficult to understand given the stated objectives of the EU in striving towards uniformity of laws within the Union. However, the disparity arises not only from differences in the legislation, but also in the basic culture and general attitudes towards privacy and reputational rights laid down in the common law and civil codes in each jurisdiction.

In a perfect world, consistent laws relating to both defamation and privacy across the Western democracies would provide a recognised approach, and more importantly the consequential ability to enforce a judgment that would be in accordance with each individual country's legislative requirements.

However, notwithstanding the clearly stated intentions behind Article 6, which was intended to grant access to justice for all under the auspices of a right to a fair trial, and taking into account the reputational and privacy protections under Article 8 and the balancing freedom of expression provided for in Article 10, the reality is, in the UK at least, these well meaning European objectives have been applied inconsistently and somewhat erratically. Perhaps one of the more significant recent decisions of the ECtHR was the ruling that the *Daily Mirror's* freedom of expression was violated by the legal costs it had to pay when it lost the privacy case brought by the supermodel Naomi Campbell. Although Ms Campbell had been successful in persuading the Law Lords that the newspaper had breached her privacy in an article about her leaving a drug rehabilitation clinic, the ECtHR ruled that the £1m legal fees the paper had to pay, which were made up partly of a "success fee", were excessive[1].

Ms Campbell's case arose from the publication in February 2001 of a report about her drug addiction, including a photograph of her leaving a Narcotics Anonymous

---

1   *MGN Limited v The United Kingdom 39401/04* [2011] ECHR 66 (18 January 2011)

meeting in London. She was initially awarded £3,500 damages for breach of privacy by the High Court but the Appeal Court subsequently over-ruled this judgment, ordering her to pay the paper's £350,000 legal costs, before that decision was ultimately overturned by the Law Lords based on breach of confidentiality and a breach of duty under the Data Protection Act 1998. The judgment left the *Mirror* facing a total legal bill of more than £1m.

The newspaper complained to the ECtHR that this decision, together with the level of legal costs, breached the newspaper's right to "freedom of expression" under the Human Rights Convention. However, the European Court rejected the former claim, stating that a balance had to be struck between *"the public interest in the publication of the articles and photographs of Ms Campbell and the need to protect her private life"*[2]. The ruling went on to state that *"Given that the sole purpose of the publication of the photographs and articles had been to satisfy the curiosity of a particular readership about the details of a public figure's private life, those publications had not contributed to any debate of general interest to society"*.[3]

In summary, the model's right to respect for her private life outweighed the protection of freedom of expression for the newspaper. Nonetheless, the ECtHR decided that the requirement to pay "success fees" was based on a UK law that had been designed to ensure the widest possible public access to legal services in civil cases, including to people who would not otherwise be able to afford a lawyer. This did not apply to Naomi Campbell, who was wealthy and therefore not lacking access to court on financial grounds.

Interestingly, the ECtHR found that there was also a risk to media reporting and freedom of expression, if the potential costs of defending a case risked putting pressure on the media and newspaper publishers to settle cases which could or should have been defended, with the Strasbourg judges finding that the requirement to pay the "success fees" was disproportionate to the aim sought to be achieved by the introduction of the system in the first place.

This decision, although on one view fair and reasonable, had the unfortunate effect of encouraging the media generally to believe that their ongoing campaign against what they regard as the unfairness of the UK libel law in general is justified. Furthermore, the general public, if not already intimidated by the intensity of the earlier press campaign against libel litigation, would have been influenced by this decision from the ECtHR, often regarded as the last bastion of protection for the man on the street.

As a consequence, we are really no further on in terms of not only consistency in the application of the law but, perhaps even more importantly, clarification as to its implementation across the board.

Just as the law of privacy has been developing in the UK based on the more controversial and contentious cases that are perhaps not representative of the more

2 Ibid para 142
3 Ibid para 143

mundane and run of the mill breaches, likewise, those cases that reach the end of the long and expensive road to the European court can also be unrepresentative and specific to "unique" aspects of the law.

Even if, by some miracle, agreement could be reached in relation to a common libel and privacy law applicable to all European Member States, the disparity with the First Amendment rights in the United States would still remain, together with the same basic problems relating to enforcement.

For instance, a pan-European law would not assist or improve on the ability to enforce against offshore ISPs or those service providers based in the sanctuary of the United States, and the fundamental cultural differences, never mind legal requirements, on each side of the Atlantic will result in the ongoing conflict of laws. The reality, of course, is that this cultural divide is not just a transatlantic one, but is equally prevalent between European countries. In France, damages for libel are comparatively modest and the law is utilised much less than in the UK, simply because of the privacy protection available. In Italy the situation is similar with an even more robust protection for celebrities and ordinary individuals against intrusions by the paparazzi, and the press in general. Perhaps this is as a result of the more liberal attitudes towards, for instance, extramarital affairs and the general conduct of politicians in both countries. These countries and the attitudes of their lawmakers towards libel and privacy are discussed in more detail later in this chapter.

Such marked divergence from the position in the UK was very clearly illustrated by the differing attitudes towards Dominique Strauss-Khan following his high profile arrest for what was ultimately found to be an unproven allegation. Even when the worldwide hysteria surrounding his arrest was at its height, in his home country of France, the reaction was comparatively muted, with indifference and lack of surprise towards a leading political figure's indiscretions – particularly given their nature. Not so in the US of course, where Strauss Kahn was filmed in handcuffs. Perhaps this incident best epitomises this particular contrast between the European and US cultures, which in turn has been encapsulated in the relevant legislation in each jurisdiction.

While we have previously touched on the general attitude towards libel and privacy in other countries, perhaps a more detailed overview is required in order to chart the extent of the divergence of views across the European and global spectrum.

France for instance has a long established history of emphatically guarding the privacy of its inhabitants. Perhaps the most well known illustration of this phenomenon concerned the child born to the mistress of Francois Mitterrand, whose existence remained a secret from the public for over two decades until his Presidency had terminated. A similar set of circumstances is impossible to envisage in the UK, where the media feels no obligation to suppress the publication of the personal affairs of politicians.

The French have historically been robustly vigilant in protecting the right to privacy. Such rights have evolved concurrently with image rights in France and the balance between freedom of speech and privacy has to date fallen squarely on the side of protection of the privacy of the individual.[4]

A notable case which underlined this position, heralding the way for more comprehensive legislative protection for privacy rights, concerned the unauthorised portrait of the 19th Century French actress known as *Mademoiselle Rachel*. The controversy arising from the portrait centred on the fact that it was taken of her when she was effectively on her deathbed. Her family's complaint was successful and the French Civil Court recognised in its judgment of 16 June 1858:

> *"...no one may, without the express consent of the family, reproduce and make available to the public the features of a person on his deathbed, however famous this person has been and however public his acts during his life have been; the right to oppose this reproduction is absolute and it should not be disregarded; otherwise the most intimate and respectable feelings would be offended."*[5]

Such pertinent words beg the question as to where UK journalists' considerations for the most "intimate and respectable of feelings" were when, at the behest of their editor, they entered the hospital room of Gordon Kaye in 1991 after he had sustained serious injuries in a car accident. They proceeded to photograph the actor, best known for his role in the comedy series *'Allo 'Allo*, despite the notices that were pinned to his door in the hospital restricting the passage of any visitors who were not either close friends or family and despite the fact that he clearly did not have capacity to consent to his photograph being taken.

An interim injunction suppressed immediate publication of the photographs, although the newspaper that planned to publish them, the *Sunday Sport* succeeded on appeal. One of the Court of Appeal judges made the following observation: "*It is well-known that in English law there is no right to privacy, and accordingly there is no right of action for breach of a person's privacy. The facts of the present case are a graphic illustration of the desirability of Parliament considering whether and in what circumstances statutory provision can be made to protect the privacy of individuals.*"[6] This statement was to serve as a bar to successful UK privacy actions for the next decade, until the introduction of the Human Rights Act and a pan-European right to privacy and family life, albeit one that had to be weighed against the right to freedom of expression.

Notwithstanding this European right, the French still appear to have a culture based on the preservation of the integrity and privacy of the individual, as opposed to providing blanket protection for the press. The underlying, domestic legislation

---

4   See Section 9 of the Civil Code (and also in criminal law, at Section 226–1 *et seq*. Of the French Criminal Code. Source: *International Libel & Privacy Handbook*, edited by Charles J Glasser, 2nd ed p293

5   The *Rachel* affaire. Judgment of 16 June 1858, Trib pr inst de la Seine, 1858 DP III 62. *See* Jeanne M Hauch, Protecting Private Facts in France: The Warren & Brandeis Tort is Alive and Well and Flourishing in Paris, 68 Tul L Rev. 1219 (May 1994) .... Sourced from: https://www.privacyinternational.org/article/france-privacy-profile.

6   *Kaye v Robertson* [1991] FSR 62

came into force in 1970 in the form of Article 9 of the Civil Code which provided that "everyone has the right to respect for their privacy". The marked difference between the French legislation and the British understanding of the laws on privacy is patently clear from the assertion in French law that public figures are equally entitled to respect for their private lives. In a 1997 case relating to Francois Mitterrand, it was held that, "...*everyone, regardless of rank, birth, wealth and present or future role in society, is entitled to have his private life respected.*[7]" Furthermore, under the Penal Code currently in force in France, anyone who is held to have infringed another's right to privacy is liable to be fined up to €45,000 in addition to the possible sanction of up to one year's imprisonment.

It has been reported that the enactment of the stringent privacy laws came about as a result of several high profile complaints emanating from none other than the globally renowned French actress, Brigitte Bardot, who sought legal intervention in respect of articles alleging that she had tried to commit suicide.

In more recent years, there have been a number of well documented cases brought by the likes of Nicolas Sarkozy, who has been continuously at loggerheads with the French press. The French President's complaints have primarily been in the sphere of privacy, and revolve mainly around the planned publication of references to his former wife, Cecilia, and details concerning their divorce. In 2006, when Sarkozy was running for President, he sought relief as a result of a publication in *Le Matin*, which he claimed violated his right to privacy[8]. The French speaking Swiss magazine was the first to disclose his separation from Cecilia, and also printed allegations that she had been having an affair whilst still married. Similar allegations, and indeed photographs, were also published in *Paris Match* at around the same time. In the latter case, it was reported that Sarkozy called for the removal of the incumbent editor from his post; a move that the press indicated that they would strongly and collectively resist. The fact that the Sarkozys had in the past openly arranged photo shoots and even spoken to the press about aspects of their domestic life was offered by the media as justification as to why they ought not to be granted a concrete right to privacy simply because their relationship had ended or they no longer required the publicity which typically accompanies "happy family" type stories in support of his election campaign.

Similar criticism was also levelled at the family of the late Francois Mitterrand upon their successful application for an injunction to suppress the publication of a book that had been written by the former President's doctor while treating him in the years and months prior to his death[9]. The injunction (eventually overturned by the European Court of Human Rights in 2004[10]) took into consideration the outrage felt by Mitterrand's family in the face of publication of what would ordinarily be information which ought not to be published on account of its self-evidently private and confidential nature. The wider criticism came about, however, as a result of the fact that Mitterrand had provided a series of health updates to the public, opening

7   *SA Editions Plon v Mitterrand*, Civ 16 July 1997, D 1997 452
8   *Nicolas S v Le Matin*, TGI Thonon Les Bains, 22 September 2006
9   As upheld by the Court of Cassation at Cass 16 July 1997
10   *Plon v France no 58148/00* – 18 May 200

the door to the argument that the information was in fact already in the public domain.

Sarkozy's name was again the subject of legal action when his former wife took steps to put a stop to the publication of a book that had been written about her by Anna Bitton which was said to contain personal and intimate details relating to her previous marriage including her detailed, and at times less than complimentary, opinions on her ex-husband[11]. Despite arguing that the conversations between herself and Bitton were privy to an obligation of confidence on the part of the author, her bid to suppress publication failed. This action came after a successful attempt made by Sarkozy himself in 2005, when the then Minister for the Interior reportedly called the publisher of the unauthorised work into his office. Subsequent reports of the event are, perhaps unsurprisingly, rather hard to find.

Sarkozy's former Presidential rival, Ségolène Royal, was also successful in two privacy infringement cases against the publishers of the well known magazine, *Paris Match*, most recently in 2009. The magazine had published allegedly stolen photographs of her walking hand and hand with a man previously unknown to the press. She stated at the time that she was "pursued and harassed" by the press at every opportunity[12].

There are further recent instances of the French cabinet invoking their laws against wayward publishers who stray from the well understood requirement to strictly stick to reporting on professional affairs as opposed to private ones. In April 2010 for example, the French Minister François Baroin, slammed *Paris Match* on account of the six-page spread that had been published about his private life. Monsieur Baroin had provisionally cooperated with the magazine in respect of its stated intentions to report on his political career. He became not only reluctant to agree but also markedly litigious once it became apparent that the real scope of the story rested on his private life and his relationship with the actress, Michelle Laroque. The article was entitled, "*The glamour couple of politics*"[13], such a label bearing little resemblance to the manner in which Baroin had anticipated being presented by the magazine. This case raises a number of important points regarding whether a line between private and personal life can effectively be drawn and if so where one stops and the other begins.

The position regarding libel in France is distinct from that of the UK in that there is no delineation between libel and slander, any instance of libel being made out by the existence of "*any allegation or imputation of a fact which is contrary to honour or to the consideration in which is held a person or institution.*"[14]

---

11   *Ciganer-Albeniz v Cremisi, Société Flammarion and Bitton*, TGI Paris, 11 January 2008, JCP 2008, Act. 66
12   "Royal attacks 'Paris Match' over photos", 27 February 2009, http://www.independent.co.uk/news/world/europe/royal-attacks-paris-match-over-photos-1633421.html
13   "Michèle Laroque François Baroin: UnAmour Qui Compte", 1 April 2010 http://www.parismatch.com/Actu-Match/Medias/Actu/Michele-Laroque-Francois-Baroin.-Un-amour-qui-compte-176851; http://www.economist.com/node/15868467
14   Section 29 of the Law of 29 July 1881. Source: *International Libel & Privacy Handbook*, edited by Charles J Glasser, 2nd ed p286

Defences to the offence (it carries criminal as well as civil sanctions) include *Exceptio Veritatis*, more commonly known as truth or justification, which can only be relied upon in respect of facts that the publisher was in receipt of in advance of publication. The French "Good Faith" defence bears a degree of similarity to the UK common law defence of Reynolds Qualified Privilege in that it requires the following criteria to be present prior to being successfully deployed, namely: (i) a degree of objectivity on the part of the author/publisher; (ii) prudence of publication (which includes checking sources properly in advance of publication); (iii) an absence of animosity on the part of the author/publisher; and (iv) a legitimate goal on the part of the author/publisher which includes not only public interest but also genuine critique on matters of artistic, literary, scientific or historic interest.[15]

In Italy the attitude of lawmakers to libel and privacy is different to the UK in that the fundamental right to privacy ranks highly amongst its fellow competing rights as it is codified in Article 2 of the Italian Constitution. Whilst it is not defined, it is loosely understood to enable all citizens to enjoy equal social dignity and a right to the protection of their honour, reputation, personality and personal image.

Italian citizens also have the clarity and protection of an enshrined Personal Data Protection Code[16], which has in recent years been the subject of a not inconsiderable degree of controversy. The Code came under scrutiny when in 2006, Google, Inc was forced to remove an online video which was reported as being offensive. The video contained footage of a young disabled boy being taunted and bullied by other children. The boy, who had Down's Syndrome was insulted repeatedly during the course of his attack and a number of vicious remarks were directed at the Italian Charity for individuals with Down's Syndrome, *Viva Down*.

Subsequent to the removal of the video from the internet, *Viva Down* argued that the boy's privacy had been breached and that the video ought not to have been uploaded in the first place, or in any event, it should have been removed after a shorter period of time. A criminal case was brought against three Google executives, all of whom were cleared of defamation but were each given a six month suspended sentence for privacy violation, the prosecutors stating that "*a company's rights cannot prevail over a person's dignity.*"[17]

A plethora of global commentary on the merits of the case quickly followed the news of the Italian Court's decision. Unsurprisingly the media was quick to criticise the finding, arguing that it was akin to prosecuting the post office in the event that hate mail managed to make its way in to a post box and that the pre-screening of online content for a media giant such as Google was simply not technically possible. Vigorous claims were immediately made on the part of Google to the effect that it intended to appeal the decision, although the outcome of any such appeal does not appear to have been reported.

---

15   Source: *International Libel & Privacy Handbook*, ibid p288
16   Legislative Decree no. 196 of 30 June 2003
17   "Google executives convicted for Italy autism video", 24 February 2010, http://www.reuters.com/article/2010/02/24/us-italy-google-conviction-idUSTRE61N2G520100224

Chapter 10 An international perspective

It is perhaps the torrent of debate surrounding the larger than life former Italian Prime Minister, Silvio Berlusconi, which has ensured that the relevancy of Italian privacy and libel laws has remained a constant item on the democratic agenda. Berlusconi has ignored the calls to hand over his share in the country's largest media organization, *Mediaset*, a step which would go some way to silencing those who accuse him of partaking in what they perceive to be a clear conflict of interest. *Mediaset* was set up by the then entrepreneur, Berlusconi in the 1970s and he still holds a majority share in the company, to the ire of his many opponents.

No stranger to controversy and criticism, Berlusconi has assisted numerous courts and tribunals with their investigations. There have been a number of charges levelled at him including false accounting, tax evasion, fraud, bribery and abuse of office, not to mention the recent claims that he paid several women in return for sexual favours. Despite the efforts of Italian prosecutors, Berlusconi remains very much at large, and prides himself on resisting the attempts to criminalise his affairs, publicly declaring that *"resistance and sacrifice will give the Italians a more fair and efficient judicial system [which] makes me even more proud"*[18]. Much of the evidence that was collated in connection with the recent sex scandals that have dogged Berlusconi was obtained, much to his indignation, by means of wire-tapping. The revelation led him to stop using his mobile phone and proclaim himself to be *"the most persecuted politician in the history of the world"*[19]. The outcome of the investigations into Berlusconi's seemingly unlawful relations with young women, one in particular who was under the age of consent at the time she was alleged to be involved in her dalliance with Berlusconi, is yet to become apparent. Berlusconi is still making regular court appearances, however, and faced difficult questions over his recorded statements to the effect that he was "just a Prime Minister in my spare time[20]" and expressing regret that his official duties got in the way of the time that he would otherwise be spending with his "babes".

When confronted with the string of newsworthy events pertaining to their Premier, it is little wonder that the Italian press does not take kindly to his attempts to silence them. In 2009 the Italian media staged a 24 hour strike in the face of Berlusconi's threats to introduce a so-called "gagging law", one of the foremost provisions of which would restrict the unauthorised recording of telephones and other electronic devices by the authorities. The restriction entailed the cumbersome proviso that in order to be permitted to wire-tap, those seeking to do so would require the advance permission from three separate judges in order to keep themselves on the right side of the law. A further condition stipulated the prohibition of the publication of any transcripts that resulted from the wire-tapping of phones. According to the proposed reforms, only cases relating to the mafia or to terrorism would be exempt from its provisions.

18 "Judges urged to jail Berlusconi", 12 November 2004, http://news.bbc.co.uk/1/hi/world/europe/4007441.stm
19 Berlusconi "most persecuted man", 9 October 2009, http://news.bbc.co.uk/1/hi/8300184.stm
20 Berlusconi allegedly said this to businessman Gianpaolo Tarantini: "Italy Scandal: Silvio Berlusconi in 'sex boast'", 17 September 2011, http://www.bbc.co.uk/news/world-europe-14960214

More recently, in October 2011 Wikipedia temporarily pulled its Italian site, www. wikipedia.it, from the internet, amidst concerns that, as part of the proposed reforms, Berlusconi's government intended to legislate on the issue of online publication of material that could be construed as offensive or a violation of privacy. The new legislation will, if passed, oblige online publishers to remove material that has been complained of within 48 hours of receiving the complaint. They will additionally have to publish a correction and they will not be able to avail themselves of any process of appeal. The law, which is currently in draft form, is required to protect the privacy rights of Italian citizens, according to Berlusconi. Mass protests have been staged, particularly in Rome, by those who are convinced that the proposed legislative reforms are simply a bid to suppress honest reporting and an attempt to gag stories about Berlusconi and his flamboyant lifestyle.

As regards the libel laws currently in force in Italy, the provisions are enshrined in the Constitution, which as we have already seen, specifically protects the right to a reputation. As is the case with privacy, such right has to be balanced with the right to freedom of speech, although it has been demonstrated to some extent that the right to reputation, image, honour and privacy are deemed to have a superior status to that of freedom of expression[21].

Alongside the defence of truth, those who are accused of publishing defamatory material are able to avail themselves of the defence of good faith in appropriate circumstances, namely when the communication is not couched in abrasive terms and it has been made in the public interest. Such a defence will typically only be deployed when the offending or incorrect material is objective and does not ride roughshod over the dignity of its subject.

The controversial criminal case of Amanda Knox and Raffaele Sollecito gave rise to the Italian courts consideration of sanctions that ought to be imposed in cases of defamation. Knox had, in the course of the investigation into the murder of Meredith Kercher, been charged with slander in claiming that her employer, Patrick Lumumba, was guilty of the murder, and also that she had been the victim of police brutality. Knox was convicted on a charge of slander at her original trial for the murder of her former flatmate, and although acquitted of the murder charge on appeal, received a three year prison sentence and fine of €22,000 on the separate slander conviction. She had however already served four years of her original sentence before her acquittal in the murder charge, therefore did not have to serve any additional time in prison for the charges that were upheld against her for slander[22].

The way in which private information is stored by online and other organisations has also sounded several notes of concern throughout Europe in recent times. One organisation in particular, *Europe versus Facebook*, has entreated watchdogs to monitor the way in which individuals' data is recorded and used by the online giant. Much is being made by the Austrian based organisation of the fact that Facebook

---

21   Source: *International Libel & Privacy Handbook*
22   "Amanda Knox Wins Meredith Kercher Murder Appeal", 4 October 2011, BBC (http://www.bbc. co.uk/news/world-europe-15158163)

now owns a company which is registered in Ireland, the argument being that since it is based there and its users accordingly contract with an Irish organisation when using the site, that *Facebook* ought to be bound by the laws of the State from which it is operating. Whilst such discussions are still very much in the academic stages, the Irish Data Protection Commissioner has been asked to respond to a number of complaints directly related to the purported ill-use of information which has been garnered by *Facebook* without the implicit knowledge or consent of its users. Whatever the outcome of these types of complaints, it will presumably not be long until the relatively new Irish Privacy Bill[23] is deployed in response to online users' gripes in connection with the storage of their personal data. It will certainly be interesting to see how the judiciary and legal watchdogs handle the ever changing role of technology in society when it comes to enforcing the law.

Furthermore, recent discussions with *Twitter* and the Irish government on the subject of Twitter opening a Dublin-based operation, will perhaps keep these types of issues on the debating agenda for parliamentary lawmakers across Europe.

Citizens of European Member States have now been able to enjoy the protection laid down in the Convention on Human Rights for many years. Since coming into force, courts across Europe have wrestled with the balancing exercises that necessarily come with the territory of interpreting this instrument. It remains to be seen whether there will ever effectively be a unified code in the cases of privacy and reputational legislation, although at the moment it is abundantly clear that any universal agreement on these types of issues is very unlikely to materialise. In the meantime, it will be interesting to monitor the judicial decisions in the struggle between privacy and press freedom, in the hope that a balance can be found in relation to what has been a longstanding and controversial source of contention.

---

23   Privacy Bill 2006 (http://www.oireachtas.ie/documents/bills28/bills/2006/4406/b4406s.pdf)

Chapter 11

Intellectual property and other rights

"Death is not the end. There remains the litigation over the Estate".

(Ambrose Bierce)

Of course privacy and libel are not the only areas where there is a contrasting approach by legislators and the judiciary on either side of the Atlantic. In the US for instance, there is a defined image right which is protected by the law in life and death, whereas in the UK no such right exists, but as in the case of privacy, the law is being gradually developed through the Courts. In addition, there is also significant divergence between the approach to image rights in the UK and other European jurisdictions.

With regard to what is commonly known as "a right to publicity" is concerned in the UK, the unauthorised use of a well known person's image for commercial purposes is allowed provided the impression is not given that the product or service is authorised or endorsed by the celebrity. In this day and age, international personalities can earn significant sums from the use of their name, characteristics and fame by way of advertising and commercial endorsements, but there is little they can do, in the UK at least, to prevent others from deriving the same benefit from unauthorised use of their image.

However, with the branding of the footballer David Beckham[1] being a prime example of the vast potential earnings from celebrity endorsements, sales of counterfeit goods can have significant ramifications for not only the celebrity himself, but also the product they are endorsing. In the absence of any actual law of publicity, as with privacy, high profile individuals have been seeking protection from the courts using the established laws of defamation, confidentiality, malicious falsehood and the various statutory Advertising Codes and Regulations, specifically those applying to intellectual property rights.

The Advertising Standards Codes, including the CAP Code for non broadcast advertising and the BCAP Code for TV and radio advertising, offer a degree of protection for those individuals whose images have been used in advertisements or

---

1   Beckham regularly tops the list of the highest paid sports personalities with a significant proportion of his income attributable to sponsorship deals. http://www.guardian.co.uk/football/2010/apr/22/david-beckham-wealth

for promotional purposes without their consent. Complaints can be made to the Advertising Standards Agency (ASA), which has the power to ask the advertiser to withdraw or change the offending advertisement. However, the sanctions available to the ASA are limited in scope and if an advertiser refuses to comply the matter must be then referred to the Office of Fair Trading (OFT).

Trade mark law[2] offers a viable means of protecting image rights and a number of celebrities have registered their names as Community Trade Marks (CTM) in order to commercially exploit the value in their name while at the same time preventing its use by anyone else. Globally renowned sport stars such as Tiger Woods and Wayne Rooney have registered their names as Community Trade Marks (ie protected throughout the European Community) in relation to a wide range of branded products including sportswear, fragrances etc. Any marks which are "distinctive" may be capable of being registered as trademarks. These can include names, an individual's likeness, signature or catchphrase, and application can be made to extend this protection globally by registering an International Trade Mark.

In addition to copyright and trademark protection, the tort of *passing off* protects individuals against the appropriation of another person's identity. The UK Courts have also recognised character merchandise as attracting protection under this aspect of the law. For an individual to succeed in an action for passing off, both parties must be in a trade or business and there must be a misrepresentation to the public leading them to believe that the goods are those of a particular individual and that as a result the individual has suffered damage.

Attempts have been made to protect personality rights following the incorporation of the European Convention of Human Rights into UK law. The landmark case brought by former Formula One racing driver Eddie Irvine against Talksport Ltd[3] provided some further clarification on existing law by addressing the protection of the celebrity against false endorsement of a product that they would have been morally opposed to endorsing (such as a tobacco product) in the first place, or where such an endorsement could prejudice an existing contract with a current sponsor. In this case, Eddie Irvine's photograph had been legitimately licensed from a photograph library by the defendants although their liability resulted from a rather unwise decision to doctor the image and emblazon "*Talk Radio*" (as it was then called), alongside the image, giving the false impression that Irvine had sanctioned the advertisement.

Irvine was awarded £2,000 in damages at the initial Hearing, although this was increased to £25,000 on appeal. It was found that, at the time, Irvine had considerable goodwill and was accordingly entitled to prevent others from making a commercial gain by holding themselves out as having been endorsed by him. The legal requirement for the two parties to be engaged in the same field of commercial activity was in this case deemed to be unnecessary to uphold a claim for passing off, since the defendants had clearly delivered a misleading message which had the

2   Trade Marks Act 1994
3   *Edmund Irvine & Tidswell Ltd v Talksport Ltd* [2003] EWCA Civ 423

desired effect on the general public. In other words, they would have taken Irvine as having backed the company when he in fact had done nothing of the sort, nor had he been paid what would otherwise have been a substantial fee to have done so.

In light of the above it must be conceded that the landscape of UK law regarding the protection of image and personality rights is not entirely bleak. Since the incorporation of the ECHR we have seen incremental movements in UK law towards affording greater protection to personality rights under the auspices of Article 8. As illustrated in *Douglas v Hello*[4] and *Campbell v MGN*[5], image rights have been given a degree of protection. The underlying concepts of this protection have also been transposed to the area of criminal justice as *Venables & Thompson v News Group Newspapers Ltd*[6] demonstrated. This case concerned the release of two juveniles who had been convicted of the murder of two year old James Bulger. Given the notoriety of the murder and widespread public outrage, the Court granted a *contra mundum* injunction to prevent any publication of their images (or indeed any other identifying information) on the basis that publication of this nature may put their lives at risk. Whatever the merits of this highly emotive and ground breaking decision, it represented a significant extension of the law of breach of confidence towards a new law of privacy.

However, notwithstanding Eddie Irvine's hard won success and other lesser known victories, English law remains better known for the not so successful attempts to protect images, likenesses or other celebrity-based claims. A famous example which sought the protection of the laws of defamation where copyright could not assist, was the so-called "Madge and Harold" case in which two Australian actors, who had become well known faces in the UK on account of their star appearances in the weekly soap *Neighbours*, took umbrage at photographs of their faces being superimposed onto the bodies of two individuals who were not so concerned with the risk of sustaining damage to their reputations[7]. These individuals were almost naked and engaged in what was commonly considered to be a pornographic pose. The case gave us the now well established principle that headlines and photographs cannot be read or viewed in isolation and an article can only be considered defamatory when taken as a whole and assessed in its entirety.

The goodwill element of a claim for passing off cannot be based on past glories and consumers' associations need to involve celebrities that are current and are therefore able to make financial gains on account of their fame. This principle was highlighted when the former British athlete, David Bedford, sought to complain about the use of his likeness in the now well known "118 118" television advertisements. Ofcom held[8] that whilst the adverts did in fact caricature Mr Bedford with his trademark moustache and 70s-style running attire and were thus in breach of the Ofcom

---

4   [2007] UKHL 21: [2005] EWCA CIV 595, [2005] EWCA CIV 861
5   [2004] UKHL 22
6   (2001) 2 WLR 1038 : (2001) 1 FLR 791 : (2001) UKHRR 628
7   *Charleston & Smith v News Group Newspapers Ltd* [1995] 2 AC 65
8   Outcome of appeal by The Number (UK) Ltd regarding complaint by David Bedford, 27 January 2004 (http://stakeholders.ofcom.org.uk/enforcement/advertising-complaints-bulletins/appeal-the-number-david-bedford/)

Code, nonetheless they would not adjudicate that the advertisements be banned. The basis for their reasoning was that Bedford had not suffered any financial loss as a result of the advertisements and an enforced ban would be disproportionate to any harm caused to him, particularly on account of the vast sums of money that the makers of the adverts had poured into their campaign by the time Mr. Bedford's complaint was received.

For those individuals who are not in the public eye but nevertheless find that their image has been used without their consent, it appears that the best form of recourse is available to them is the provisions of the Data Protection Act 1998 (DPA). Pursuant to s 1(1) of the DPA such images may amount to *personal data* ie such data which relates to a living person who can be identified, or they may on some occasions constitute *sensitive personal data* ie if they reveal sensitive information such as an individual's race, religion, political beliefs, health or sexual orientation.

In contrast to the position in the UK, the protection of privacy, personality and image rights are the object of strict regulation in France, while there is the familiar acknowledgement of the right of free enterprise and the freedom of expression on the one hand and the protection of the aforesaid personality rights on the other. The right to privacy in France is enshrined within Article 9 of the *Code Civil*[9], and the stringent protection it provides was aptly demonstrated in 2008 when controversial low budget airline Ryanair used images of the President Nicolas Sarkozy and his then girlfriend, the model/singer Carla Bruni, in an advertisement published in *Le Parisen*. The ad featured a photograph of the couple with a speech caption beside Ms Bruni proclaiming, *"With Ryanair, my whole family can come to my wedding"*[10]. The couple filed separate lawsuits against the airline for the unauthorised use of their images with Ms Bruni claiming €500,000 Euro in compensation (allegedly the cost of publishing authorised photos of the model) while the President sought €1 in damages. The court ruled in favour of the couple awarding Ms Bruni €60,000 in compensation, with the President receiving the symbolic €1 damages he requested[11]. Ryanair were also ordered by the court to publish the verdict in the newspaper which carried the original advertisement. In addition, in a novel case heard in November 2010, the *Tribunal de Grande Instance de Paris* awarded damages for infringement of image rights arising out of the Defendant's creation of a fake Facebook profile in the Plaintiff's name and illustrated with his photograph[12]. The Plaintiff, who is a comedian and entertainer, claimed that this webpage constituted a violation of his privacy as well his image rights. The Court held that photographs of the Plaintiff could not be published in this manner without his consent and awarded him €1,500 in damages.

---

9   http://www.legifrance.gouv.fr/affichCodeArticle.do?idArticle=LEGIARTI000006419288

10   "Nicolas Sarkozy threatens to sue Ryanair", *The Telegraph*, 23 January 2008, (http://www.telegraph.co.uk/news/worldnews/1576857/Nicolas-Sarkozy-threatens-to-sue-Ryanair.html)

11   *N Sarkozy v Sté Ryanair* and *C Bruni Tedeschi v Sté Ryanair*, TGI Paris, 5 February 2008, JCP 2008, Act. 117. ; "Sarkozy and Bruni win Ryanair payout," *The Guardian*, 5 February 2008 (http://www.guardian.co.uk/media/2008/feb/05/medialaw.advertising); and from Ryanair's own website: (http://www.ryanair.com/en/news/gen-en-310108)..

12   Omar S. / Alexandre P. » (TGI Paris, 17e Ch. civ., 24 novembre 2010). http://www.legalis.net/spip.php?page=jurisprudence-decision&id_article=3042

There are similarly robust protections for image rights in Germany, where a general right of personality has been held to emanate from Articles 1[13] and 2[14] of the German Constitution (*Grundgesetz*). Infringement of this personality right gives rise to a remedy under the Civil Code entitling the injured party to seek an injunction and/ or damages. German Courts have tended to take a proactive stance in upholding this right and this approach was demonstrated in 2006 when former Wimbledon champion Boris Becker was awarded €1.2m in damages after a German newspaper used his image as part of a promotional campaign without his consent.

The Italian approach to image rights also merits some consideration in analysing the evolution of these rights on the European stage. Article 10 of the Italian Civil Code expressly allows an individual (or indeed his relatives or descendants) to take steps to protect his image from being used in a way which damages his reputation. This protection is complemented by Article 96 of Copyright Law[15] which prohibits showing, reproducing or profiting from the image of an individual without their consent. An individual whose rights have been infringed in this matter will be entitled to damages under civil law and in some cases the offender may be subject to criminal sanctions under the Italian Penal Code[16]. Clearly this provides an incentive for the person wishing to use the image to seek consent.

In light of the statutory protections outlined above it certainly appears that in the European context, the UK is very much in the minority in failing to directly and comprehensively address the issue of image rights.

In the United States, a distinction is drawn between the unauthorised use of an individual's image or commercial endorsement, which is protected, and the use by a newspaper of the same picture to illustrate an article about the person which would not be deemed to violate their rights.

Interestingly, and in stark contrast to the apparent ambivalence to the fallout from reputational damage in the United States, their right of publicity laws seek to protect persons from the anguish and loss of dignity that may arise from the unauthorised use of their identity, as well as protecting the proprietary rights in an image.

The concept of a "right to publicity" as distinct from the right to privacy was first recognised in the US in the 1953 case *Haelan Laboratories v Topps Chewing Gum Inc*[17]. The plaintiff in this case was a manufacturer of chewing gum which had signed contracts with various baseball players for the exclusive rights to use their image to promote sales of the product via baseball trading cards. The defendant, a competitor of the plaintiff, also induced these sportsmen to enter into contracts allowing the defendant to use their photographs to sell its particular brand of

---

13 "The human dignity is inviolable. Any state authority is obliged to respect and protect it"
14 Everyone has the right to the free development of his personality insofar as he does not violate the rights of others or offend against the constitutional order or the moral code
15 Law for the Protection of Copyright and Neighbouring Rights (Law No 633 of April 22, 1941) art 96
16 Codice Penale [Cp] art 594, 595
17 202 F2d 866 (2d Cir)

chewing gum. Of note is the fact that the Court held that the players involved had a right to the value of the publicity attached to their photograph. The Court famously stated that: *"...a man has a right in the publicity value of his photograph, i., the right to grant the exclusive privilege of publishing his picture..."*[18] Since this seminal case publicity rights have been recognised by numerous US states whether expressly in state statutory instruments or by virtue of common law developments.

Unsurprisingly, California[19] and New York[20], being the centres of the film and broadcasting industries, have considerably more advanced publicity laws than other States. While the federal Lanham Act[21] (alternatively known as the Trademark Act), prohibiting the use in commerce of symbols or devices likely to deceive consumers as to the sponsorship of goods or services by another person[22], has been applied to false endorsement claims. The protection afforded to an identity is extended beyond the person himself to assignees, licensees or their heirs in title, with injunctions and damages being the primary remedies available from the Courts. Interestingly, a number of states also recognise the continuation of these rights beyond the lifetime of the individual for a prescribed period of time varying from 20 to 100 years after the death of the individual. This also raises a number of challenging questions about the calculation of the potential earning power of such intangible rights for the purposes of assessing inheritance tax liability.

Case law in this area has determined that an individual's image is not restricted to photographs and can include their likeness, voice, as well as their physical mannerisms and even their catchphrases.

Furthermore, a number of states also recognise the continued existence of image rights beyond the lifetime of the person. In a number of high profile cases the estates of deceased persons have been able to take legal action to prevent the exploitation of publicity rights on the basis that such rights had automatically transferred to them on death as part of the deceased's property. The Californian Civil Code[23] recognises the enforceability of publicity rights for a period of up to 70 years after the personality's death. In 2007, Governor Arnold Schwarzenegger amended[24] the Civil Code to extend this protection to persons who died before 1984. However in contrast to the generous recognition afforded in California, in 2007 a New York District Court refused to recognise that the estate of Marilyn Monroe had the right to enforce her post mortem right to publicity holding that the Hollywood Star's right to publicity had been extinguished at the time of her death in 1962 and she could not therefore devise it in her will[25]. In the aftermath of this controversial decision a lobbying campaign led by those companies holding the licensing rights to the images of various dead celebrities prompted the submission of a draft bill[26] to the

18   Ibid p868
19   Section 3344 of the California Civil Code
20   NY CLS Civ R § 50, 51 (2000)
21   15 USC
22   *International Privacy, Publicity and Personality Laws* edited by Michael Henry P447
23   California Civil Code § 3344-3344.1.
24   Bill SB 771
25   *Shaw Family Archives Ltd v CMG Worldwide*, Inc, 486 F Supp 2d 309 (SDNY 2007).
26   S06790

New York State Legislature which would amend the law to allow enforcement of a deceased personality's publicity rights up to 70 years after their death. Post mortem rights have also been recognised in some European jurisdictions most notably in Germany where the Federal Court upheld post mortem protection of personality rights in a groundbreaking case in which the estate of the deceased actress Marlene Dietrich[27] was held to be entitled to restrain the unauthorised use of Ms Dietrich's image for commercial purposes.

However, as in the law of defamation, the First Amendment creeps into the implementation of the US personality laws, on the basis that, if the law were to permit persons to control every single use of their identity, then the First Amendment and journalism itself would be totally undermined. Accordingly, a so-called "newsworthiness" privilege prevents that result. Although this privilege is a strong defence, it does have its limitations and can be rebutted. It has been rejected by US Courts on a number of occasions including the somewhat bizarre case of *Zacchini v Scripps-Howard Broadcasting Co*[28] in which the Supreme Court held that an Ohio broadcasting company was not entitled to the protection of the First Amendment after it broadcast footage of the Plaintiff's *"human cannonball"* act without his consent. The Defendants argued they were entitled to broadcast the act as it was "newsworthy". However, the Supreme Court rejected this argument and, characterising the Plaintiff's personality rights as a *proprietary right,* held that the broadcast of the entire 15-second act in its entirety had destroyed the commercial value of the act. In addition, the law will not protect "calculated falsehoods" in news reporting.

The First Amendment also provides protection in circumstances where persons are identified within the script of a novel or movie, and will bar liability for what otherwise would be a valid violation of the right of publicity. Furthermore, if a person's identity appears briefly and insignificantly, that person probably will not have a cause of action for violation of his or her right of publicity, and the "first sale doctrine" may also provide a defence to certain contended violations of the right to publicity.

In *Samuel Moore v Weinstein Company LLC*, the Plaintiff known professionally as *"The Legendary Soul Man Sam Moore"*, a former member of 1960's soul group *"Sam and Dave"*, initiated legal action against Hollywood producers Bob and Harvey Weinstein for violation of his right to publicity and exploitation of his image for commercial gain.[29] He alleged that a character in the movie *"Soul Men"* produced by the Weinstein Company was based on him. The film centred around the story of two African American soul artists whose journey around the US in the 1960s and 1970s performing *Memphis Soul* music allegedly bore considerable similarities to the real life experiences of Sam and Dave. The film also featured a number of the duo's songs.

---

27 Bundesgerichtshof [BGH-Federal Court of Justice], Case No 1 ZR 49/97, Dec 1, 1999, 143 BGHZ 214
28 433 US 562 (1977)
29 "Soul Man' sues filmmakers for depicting him," *Nashville Post,* 18 February 2009 (http://nashvillepost. com/news/2009/2/18/soul_man_sues_filmmakers_for_depicting_him)

Of interest is the fact that Moore chose to ground his cause of action in the infringement of publicity rights rather than in defamation despite the fact he claimed that the character which was based on him damaged his reputation, as the character was depicted as using racist and sexist terms, vulgar language and as being involved in violence. The grounds of complaint pleaded in this case are indicative of the inherent difficulties in bringing a defamation action in the US given the very high burden of proof imposed upon the Plaintiff and the requirement for public figures to prove malice. The Defendants for their part denied that the film is based on Mr Moore's life and moreover they claimed that even if it was, Moore is a public figure, and therefore the film would be protected by the First Amendment. However, the Defendant's attempt to have the complaint dismissed at the initial stages was rejected by a Tennessee Judge who stated that additional investigation was needed to determine whether the Plaintiff's rights had been violated or whether the Defendant's use of Moore's image should be afforded First Amendment protection[30]. The outcome of this case will be awaited with interest as it could potentially open up an alternative means of redress for those who have been misrepresented or otherwise had their reputation maligned on screen.

It remains to be seen whether the UK legislators will intervene to protect image rights in this increasingly commercial and global society. Although it is possible to obtain limited trademark protection for the signatures of individuals, the absence of any protection for wider personality rights appears indefensible in the modern area. Certainly there will be increasing pressure for a change with the ongoing globalisation of branding and other rights by virtue of the internet and extended international marketing on both products and personalities. Indeed, the general view is that as more and more jurisdictions deem themselves to be commercially at a disadvantage, change will gradually be introduced as laws become harmonised.

And of course it is not just Individuals who are being prejudiced by a lack of protection, but the multi-national music and broadcasting industry have been to the vanguard in the clamour for statutory anti-piracy protection, particularly in relation to illegal downloading of their material.

Rapid advances in technology in recent decades have brought about new opportunities for piracy. Changes in the way we consume music and other forms of digital entertainment lead to the emergence in the 1990s of peer to peer file sharing and the establishment of sites to facilitate this activity such as Napster. Long before iTunes and other online retailers began providing a legitimate method of purchasing and downloading copyrighted data, groups of internet users were engaged in illegal file sharing. As society became more technologically literate and computers fitted with high speed broadband connections became staple features in virtually every home, cases of internet piracy rose exponentially. It is estimated

---

30   *Samuel David Moore, Joyce Ellen Moore, and The SJM Trust v The Weinstein Company LLC, d/b/a/ Dimension Films, MGM Studios, Inc, Genius Products LLC, Concord Music Group LLC, Harvey Weinstein, and Bob Weinstein Case* 3:09-cv-00166 Document ·112 Filed 05/12/10, Judge Trauger (Available at: http://reporter.blogs.com/files/tnmd-16901285378.pdf; Article: http://reporter.blogs.com/ thresq/2010/05/soul-man-free-speech-lawsuit.html; Case updater at: http://dockets.justia.com/ docket/tennessee/tnmdce/3:2009cv00166/44007/)

that the music and film industries suffer billion dollar losses of revenue each year as a result of illegal downloading, and unsurprisingly they have been urging Governments to take action to curb this activity.

However, with the US still being, if not the largest, then certainly the most influential market, a question of double standards arises where on the one hand virtually unlimited First Amendment protection is being afforded to freedom of speech on the internet, while on the other there is outrage that American commercial interests are being seriously threatened as a result of the loss of income being suffered by the major music and entertainment corporations.

As in the case of privacy and defamation, harmonised international laws would appear to be the answer. Unfortunately, even if room for compromise existed in terms of the different national approaches and attitudes to such laws, then enforcement, particularly in non signatory jurisdictions, would remain virtually impossible. However, this has not prevented extensive debate on the subject and it may be that the internet itself holds the key, in terms of regulating to whom and where a service is extended.

In Ireland internet service provider Eircom launched a "three strikes" scheme to combat internet piracy after it was sued by the Irish Recorded Music Association (IRMA) for failing to protect the intellectual property of its members. The system which was initiated in May 2010 targets those who illegally download or share copyrighted material online. The system operates with the assistance of a net monitoring firm which is employed to trawl file sharing sites and identify net pirates. As the name suggests there are three phases of sanctions: in the first instance net pirates will receive a warning letter and a follow up phone call from Eircom, if they persist with this activity their internet service will be cut off for one week and if they are identified as being engaged in piracy on a third occasion their broadband service will be terminated for one year.

IRMA also issued legal proceedings against other Irish internet service providers in a bid to force them to adopt a similar system. In October 2010, the High Court in Dublin held that it could not force the service provider UPC to adopt a "three strikes approach" to illegal file sharers. As a result of this decision, the long term viability of this scheme is unclear, as the lack of a uniform approach will limit the effectiveness of the system and legislative intervention may still be required. Indeed, the Irish Government has indicated that while it would prefer a negotiated settlement between the various parties, if this is not forthcoming, legislation may yet be introduced.

Similar schemes have also been tested in other jurisdictions. In October 2009 the French Constitutional Court approved the adoption of a "three strikes" law.[31] This law created a new agency, the somewhat bizarrely entitled *High Authority of*

---

31 "Décision No. 2009-590 DC du 22 octobre 2009" (http://www.conseil-constitutionnel.fr/conseil-constitutionnel/francais/les-decisions/2009/decisions-par-date/2009/2009-590-dc/decision-n-2009-590-dc-du-22-octobre-2009.45986.html).

Diffusion of the Art Works and Protection of Rights on the Internet[32] (or "Hadopi"). Hadopi is empowered to send out warning letters and impose sanctions, including fines or the withdrawal of internet service, in respect of those individuals who are found to be deemed to be illegally sharing files. However, in order to protect free speech, the Constitutional Court ruled that the agency cannot unilaterally act to remove internet access and judicial approval must be obtained before an account can be suspended. While reaction to this scheme in France has been mixed, the agency's most recent annual report, published in October 2011[33], indicates that it has been vigorously pursuing offenders. The report reveals that 650,000 individuals have received a first strike written warning, while 44,000 have progressed to a second warning and there are 60 offenders who may be in danger of having their internet access suspended[34].

In the UK too there have been legislative attempts to combat piracy and reverse the losses suffered by the music and film industries relating to the illegal downloading of music and film content. The most significant of these measures was the long awaited the Digital Economy Act 2010 (DEA)[35]. This controversial Act, which has only partially come into force[36], contains provisions aimed at preventing illegal file sharing online. It envisages collaboration between Ofcom and the various ISP's under the umbrella of a new code of conduct which will enable the offending parties to be identified and sanctioned. In a similar fashion to the schemes in operation in Ireland and France, the Act may require ISP's to send written warnings to the offending subscribers and if these individuals continue to illegally download their service may be limited or completely suspended. However, the proposed enforcement measures have not yet been introduced. Their full implementation will be dependent on Ofcom producing an acceptable code of conduct to operate under the legislation. The Regulator released its first draft of the code in May 2010[37], which received marked criticism from ISPs[38]. This has perhaps been a contributing factor in a notable stalling of the process after publication of the first draft, where there has been no indication as to when the consultation process will be continued[39].

There are also concerns over proposals to block the content of certain websites which provide copyright free material, as some ISP's have suggested that this is extremely difficult to enforce and could lead to legitimate websites being

32 Official French title: Haute Autorite pour la Diffusion des Oeuvres et la Protection des Droits sur Internet
33 HADOPI > Rapport d'activité 2010 (http://www.hadopi.fr/sites/default/files/page/pdf/rapport-d-activite-hadopi.pdf)
34 "France acts against net pirates", *BBC*, 6 October 2011 (http://www.bbc.co.uk/news/technology-15198093)
35 2010 Chapter 24 (http://www.legislation.gov.uk/ukpga/2010/24/contents)
36 The Act came into force subject to the exceptions for Commencement as set out in Section 47 of the 2010 Act, on 8 July 2010 (http://www.legislation.gov.uk/ukpga/2010/24/section/47)
37 Online Infringement of Copyright and the Digital Economy Act 2010, Ofcom (http://stakeholders. ofcom.org.uk/binaries/consultations/copyright-infringement/summary/condoc.pdf)
38 "Digital Economy Act: ISPs criticise Ofcom code for 'distorting the broadband market,'" *The Telegraph*, 1 June 2010 (http://www.telegraph.co.uk/technology/news/7793445/Digital-Economy-Act-ISPs-criticise-Ofcom-code-for-distorting-the-broadband-market.html)
39 There had been no further consultation since the release of the first draft at the time of print

blocked. ISP's have also voiced concerns that they are being forced into the role of monitoring the internet, while online freedom campaigners have protested at the introduction of what they perceive as draconian restrictions on the exchange of information. The Department for Culture, Media and Sport, in conjunction with Ofcom, have conducted several reviews of its feasibility and operation[40]. In addition, the legislation has also been the subject of an ultimately unsuccessful[41] judicial review challenge by *Talk Talk* and *BT* on the basis that, by adopting such wide ranging anti-piracy laws, Parliament had acted *ultra vires*[42].

Although this intervention has not had a dramatic impact, with enforcement again being the problem, it does indicate that Governments and major corporations are now beginning to experiment with positive preventative steps as a means of at least testing how or whether the rampant worldwide piracy and plagiarism of material can be managed to some extent. There has been some degree of movement towards greater international co-operation to combat these violations. An international treaty on intellectual property infringement known as the *Anti-Counterfeiting Trade Agreement* (ACTA) which aims to harmonize international standards of enforcement and improve global co-operation to tackle the growing problem of IP rights, including digital copyright, has been proposed and the text of the agreement is currently in the process of being debated and ratified by each of the contracting states. A number of countries including Australia, Canada, Switzerland, Japan, the European Union and the United States were involved in the intensive negotiations surrounding the drafting of the Treaty[43].

While these developments are encouraging, only time will tell whether such pro-active steps on the international scene can be effectively implemented and enforced.

---

40   See "Next steps for implementation of the Digital Economy Act", Department for Culture, Media and Sport August 2011 (http://www.culture.gov.uk/images/publications/Next-steps-for-implementation-of-the-Digital-Economy-Act.pdf); "Impact Assessment of draft SI 'The online infringement of copyright (Initial Obligations) (Sharing of Costs) Order 2011'", Department for Culture, Media and Sport, 29 June 2011;

41   "Filesharing: BT and TalkTalk fail in challenge to Digital Economy Act," *The Guardian*, 20 April 2011 (http://www.guardian.co.uk/technology/2011/apr/20/filesharing-bt-talktalk-digital-economy-act)

42   "BT and TalkTalk granted judicial review of Digital Economy Act," *The Guardian*, 10 November 2010 (http://www.guardian.co.uk/technology/2010/nov/10/bt-talktalk-digital-economy-act)

43   "ACTA was negotiated by Australia, Canada, European Union, Japan, Mexico, Morocco, New Zealand, Republic of Korea, Singapore, Switzerland and the United States. The UK contributed to the EU negotiating position and is represented in the negotiations by the European Commission and the EU Presidency." Source: Intellectual Property Office (http://www.ipo.gov.uk/pro-policy/pro-crime/pro-crime-acta.htm)

Chapter 12

Who guards the guardians?

"There are laws to protect the freedom of the press's speech, but none
that are worth anything to protect the people from the press".

(Mark Twain)

As the initial drama arising from the 2011 phone hacking scandal began to subside, the words "public interest" began to emerge in various articles appearing in the broadsheets. The general view remained that investigative journalism performs a fundamental role in providing society with information about not only public figures, Government officials and high profile individuals, but also as a means of reporting on inappropriate or criminal conduct, albeit with the price of intrusions into aspects of private life.

Running parallel with these arguments of course is the public's insatiable appetite for gossip and scandal of a more provocative nature, which also provides sufficient commercial incentive to the more unscrupulous elements of the tabloid press. The question therefore will be who draws the line as to what is acceptable in either of these scenarios and, just as importantly, who should be entrusted with the responsibility of establishing that line in the sand?

As John Lloyd in the *Comment* section of the *Financial Times* (16 September 2011) wryly observed:

"*The late News of the World was our most popular newspaper for a reason. The Sun now holds that title.*"[1]

The popularity of these particular tabloids not only highlights what the public wants in a newspaper, but may also explain why the reaction to the phone hacking scandal has been comparatively muted since the initial outcry back in July 2011. Perhaps the public does not want a powerful, independent regulatory body controlling the press, not because they admire the often courageous work of some of our more reputable investigative journalists, but rather because they want to read the gossip in all its glory, whether it be the sexual shenanigans of a Premier League footballer or the corrupt dealings of their local Member of Parliament.

---

1   "Tame raunchy tabloids and media hit men," *Financial Times*, 16 September 2011, http://www. ft.com/cms/s/0/4f852550-df03-11e0-9af3-00144feabdc0.html#axzz1cMFsGGhe

Chapter 12 Who guards the guardians?

Lord Justice Leveson asked the question, while preparing to launch his Inquiry, as to *"Who guards the guardians?"* The UK is not the only country to allow regulation of the press. France has historically adopted a *laissez-faire* approach to media governance. The French press is not supervised by a regulatory body; instead journalists are expected to abide by the code of conduct adopted by the journalist's union – *Syndicat National des Journalistes* (SNJ) in 1918. Individual newspapers also have their own ethical codes with which their journalists are expected to comply. The fact that this hands-off approach appears to work successfully in France is arguably due in no small measure to the robust privacy protections enshrined in Article 9 of the *Code Civil.*[2]

Lessons can perhaps also be learned from the system in operation in the Republic of Ireland, where the Defamation Act 2009 established a twofold system of a Press Council working in tandem with the Press Ombudsman to oversee ethical and professional standards in the Irish press. The Press Council is wholly independent from both the government and the media and has been endowed with regulatory powers for newspapers and magazines. It is responsible for ensuring that press compliance with the Code of Practice for Newspapers and Magazines. Unlike the PCC the Irish Press Council has a fairly balanced composition with its representatives coming from various sectors of Irish society, albeit including several representatives of the newspaper industry.

The Press Ombudsman is appointed by the Press Council and has power to receive and adjudicate on complaints made by members of the public. Complaints are dealt with in accordance with the Code of Practice for Newspapers and Magazines. The Ombudsman has the discretion to refer complex complaints to the Press Council. Another level of oversight and protection for complainants is provided by the fact that any decision of the Ombudsman can be appealed to the Press Council.

Against a background of total opposition from the news industry to any form of full statutory regulation in the UK, what options are available to the Government in circumstances where, notwithstanding the ongoing scandals, there would still be a desire not to alienate the press from either the political parties or individual MPs?

Certainly, if the public is to be offered any confidence building measures, then a starting point must be to ensure that any regulatory body is made up of independent and open minded individuals, who would be prepared to act impartially and robustly. They should also bear in mind that their actions will represent a potentially significant saving on legal costs if they present themselves as a viable option to the Courts, while also acting as a deterrent against future defamatory publications and improper breaches of the right to privacy and confidentiality of the individual. It could be argued that this is hardly rocket science. Perhaps the original structure of the PCC remains a good starting point, provided those appointed to uphold this vital front line task are perceived, notwithstanding any good intentions on the part of the previous incumbents, to act decisively and with overt impartiality.

2   http://www.legifrance.gouv.fr/affichCodeArticle.do?idArticle=LEGIARTI000006419288

At the same time, one would expect the Government to move aggressively to split up the type of media empires that exist in the UK and Ireland, (and indeed in the US as well), which can only serve to undermine free speech and the credibility of what have always been among the most respected broadsheets in the world.

In an industry that is facing commercial pressures all round, whether from internet publications or the decline in traditional advertising, it should be more important than ever that the mainstream press distinguishes itself from its online competitors by ensuring that truth and accuracy represents the basic standard in their profession.

In this regard, John Lloyd in the aforementioned *Financial Times* article makes another very valid point in relation to the need to ensure that top quality investigative journalists are properly rewarded and incentivised, and that all appropriate steps are taken to ensure their independence from the press barons, some of whom have been historically criticised for interfering with the freedom of the press in a much more widespread and detrimental manner than the libel laws that have come under such intense attack in their newspapers.

The origins of the Press Complaint Commission (PCC) can be traced back to the first regulatory body for the British press, the Press Council, a voluntary organisation that was formed in 1953 for the maintenance of ethical standards in Journalism and for the promotion of press freedom. In reality it was a belated response to recommendations by a Royal Commission of 1949. Due to crucial failings of several newspapers in this regard in the 1980s, Parliament and select members of the press lost confidence in the Council, prompting consideration of the establishment of a legislative regulatory framework. What followed was a review carried out by a Departmental Committee led by David Calcutt QC to consider the best way forward for press regulation. Published in June 1990, Calcutt's report recommended the establishment of a Press Complaints Commission instead of the implementation of any legislative based regime. This was obviously largely favoured by the press, which wished to remain free of any strict legal standards. The new Press Complaints Commission was given 18 months to prove its worth before a statutory system for press complaints would be introduced if it were to fail. The PCC took shape at the start of 1991, later publishing its first formal Code of Practice, which it should be noted was established exclusively by national and regional press editors in the first instance. The PCC in time came to be funded by a the Press Standards Board of Finance (PSBF), which enlisted subscription fees from members of the industry, i.e. the publications that were supposedly to be regulated under the scheme, by way of funding. The issue of the industry being entirely self-regulated has been touched upon previously in the book.

However, there is no doubt that the principle of self-funding and self-regulation is held up as a standard for freedom of expression and freedom of the press, by that very same industry. The PCC's website selectively quotes former Minister for Culture, Media and Sport, Margaret Hodge MP, of the previous Labour Government, stating in December 2007:

Chapter 12 Who guards the guardians?

"The Government strongly supports freedom of speech and a free press. It is therefore appropriate that there should be a system of self-regulation. We are generally satisfied that the Press Complaints Commission's Code of Practice is both adequate and appropriate for its purpose."[3]

There is another well-chosen quote from Prime Minister, David Cameron MP in his speaking to the Press Gazette in April 2008, published with the PCC's ambit:

"We've no plans to change self-regulation. I think the PCC has settled down and the system is now working better that it once did. But that is not to say that there isn't an ongoing need to make sure the press acts responsibly."[4]

As a self-regulating body, the PCC counts many leading media figures among its ranks. The current members of the Commission include Ian MacGregor, Editor of the *Sunday Telegraph*, John McLellan, Editor of *The Scotsman*, Lindsay Nicholson, Editorial Director of *Good Housekeeping*, Simon Reynolds, Editorial Director of *the Lancashire Evening Post*, Tina Weaver, Editor of the *Sunday Mirror*, and Peter Wright, Editor of the *Mail on Sunday,* as well as a selection of members with no association with the press.

In February 2010, the House of Commons Culture, Media and Sport (CMS) Committee published a report on press standards, privacy and libel[5]. The enquiry, as the paper states, was primarily prompted by the persistent disparaging of Kate and Gerry McCann by the UK press after the abduction of their daughter, Madeleine, in Portugal in May 2007. Unsurprisingly, in that case the Committee recognised that there had been limited intervention of the PCC, which had failed to launch an enquiry into the industry's response in the wake of what were outrageous allegations about the family. Another notable failing of the PCC occurred in 2009, when the regulator failed to take action against newspapers that had broken the PCC code of practice in a scandal exposed in a documentary showing that various of the "red-top" UK tabloids had taken measures to obtain private medical records, before running entirely bogus stories on celebrities such as Amy Winehouse, Pixie Geldoff and Guy Ritchie.

In 1993, Sir David Calcutt had published a lesser known report commissioned by the Government, concluding that self-regulation was not working and recommending that the Government should indeed impose a system of statutory regulation. For some reason however, these recommendations were not acted upon and a common theme pointing to the inherent weaknesses in the press control system had begun to emerge almost two decades ahead of the dramatic events of 2011.

While the CMS Committee acknowledged that the PCC was not a dormant body and did take measures to address various complaints, the difficulty with accepting

---

3   http://www.pcc.org.uk/about/history.html
4   Ibid
5   House of Commons, Culture, Media and Sport Committee: Press standards, privacy and libel – Second Report of Session 2009–10, London: The Stationary Office Limited, 24 February 2010 (http://www.publications.parliament.uk/pa/cm200910/cmselect/cmcumeds/362/362i.pdf)

the statistics from what could appear, superficially, as an effective medium for addressing complaints against the press was summarized in the following quote from the Committee's report:

"There is no doubt that the PCC does a great deal of valuable work both in preventing breaches of the code and in addressing complaints and we note that the PCC is successful as a mediator. The figures show that many people have benefited from a free and discrete service in exactly the way the PCC's founders envisaged we wish to commend the staff of the PCC for this work. However, in the evidence presented to our enquiry, the general effectiveness of the PCC has been repeatedly called into question..."[6]

One particular criticism was the lack of any real sanctions. Indeed, in the Committee's recounting of events surrounding the role of the PCC in the press treatment of the Madeleine McCann abduction, it was stated the McCann's were actually informed by the Chairman of the PCC, Sir Christopher Meyer, that the PCC was not really an appropriate form for disputing libels or falsehoods that were published in newspapers[7]. It was recounted that McCann's lawyer had at the same time remarked that it was useless to take up such an issue via the PCC, as it was a media friendly organization that lacked teeth[8].

When considering whether it would be appropriate for the PCC to develop a set of penalties or sanctions (such as fines), the Committee found that the PCC had rightly asserted that the reason for not doing this was essentially to keep its members paying subscription fees, a status quo that may be threatened if contributors found themselves liable to pay fines etc for any breaches of the Code of their voluntary regulator.

This is contrary to the range of powers allocated to other regulatory bodies, such as Ofcom, the statutory body charged with regulation of radio and television broadcast, which can issue fines for any breaches of its Broadcasting Code. A further comparison can be made with the Advertising Standards Authority (ASA). While it is similar to the PCC in that it is industry funded and lacks any power to impose penalties, it does have a mechanism for referral of any advertiser, agency or publisher in breach of ASA Standards to the Office of Fair Trading, or indeed it can refer the offending broadcaster directly to Ofcom. Perhaps in keeping with tradition and historical attitudes, the newspaper industry has managed to avoid the imposition of any regulation beyond that provided by the most archaic voluntary framework, established and maintained from within its own ranks like some kind of "fraternity". However, the CMS Committee appeared not to favour an approach for radical reforms, stating:

---

6   House of Commons, Culture, Media and Sport Committee: Press standards, privacy and libel – Second Report of Session 2009–10, London: The Stationary Office Limited, 24 February 2010 – p118 paras 512–513
7   Ibid p87–88 para 357
8   Ibid p88 para 358

Chapter 12 Who guards the guardians?

"We remain of the view that self-regulation of the press is greatly preferable to statutory regulation, and should continue. However for confidence to be maintained, the industry regulator must actually effectively regulate, not just mediate. The powers of the PCC must be enhanced, as it is toothless, compared to other regulators."[9]

However, granting enhanced sanctions to the PCC may be problematic, as harsher penalties may be more likely to prompt members to reconsider their voluntary commitment to the regulatory regime.

And of course the PCC has ruthlessly implemented the very subtle sanction of refusing to consider any complaint that is already the subject of legal proceedings or where legal recourse has been threatened., This often presents complainants with a dilemma because, with time often being of the essence and funding being a major consideration the PCC approach – as is its intention – can be enough to discourage litigation. The PCC would most likely argue that this is a legitimate part of its approach because it would not want to prejudice the legal process but this is not credible. There is, in reality, no reason why the subject of defamatory allegations should not be entitled to maintain a complaint against the PCC at the same time as issuing legal proceedings, with a view to achieving vindication at the earliest possible opportunity. Any clarification that a newspaper is compelled to publish as a result of an adverse PCC finding, could form part of an argument for a reduction in damages as a result of this potentially mitigating step, albeit one which the newspaper has been "compelled" to facilitate. Indeed, the Committee found that:

"In cases where there have been clear and systemic failings by the press, the PCC should not use Court proceedings as a reason not to launch its own enquiry. If the PCC were seen as more balanced and effective then it is more likely that people will wish to use its services."[10]

The Committee generally found that the PCC was widely recognized as not being independent of the press, or at least independent enough. While Baroness Buscombe, following her appointment as PCC Chair in August 2009, carried out a review aimed specifically at increasing the independent profile of the regulator, the Committee was of the view that this was nowhere near sufficient. The passive nature of the PCC was also criticised, being only set up to act on complaints from specific individuals, notwithstanding that they may have resorted to more effective means to resolve their disputes against the press, such as legal proceedings, and did not take a more proactive approach to the maintenance of standards or adherence to its own Code by its own members. Essentially there is no preventative deterrent element built into the PCC Code or mandate. It was at least recognized that the resignation of Peter Hill, Editor of the *Daily Express*, from the PCC board in May 2008 and refusal of the Express Group Newspapers to contribute to subscription fees as of December 2007, exposed a weakness in the very principle of the self-

9   Ibid p121 para 531
10   Ibid p123 para 539

regulation system. It was held that, in reality, there was an absence of any incentive for subscription to the PCC, leaving a very precarious system in place as what was supposedly the sole arbiter of the industry's standards.

A further difficulty highlighted was the PCC's apparent inability to enforce the publication of apologies of comparable prominence to the offending article, as was evident by the tendency of publishers to afford as little print space to apologies as possible. The final recommendation of the Committee was that for serious breaches of the Editorial Code, the PCC should have the ability to impose a financial penalty. The Committee believed that this would be possible without installing a statutory framework behind the PCC, but that this could be a form of enhancing the PCC's credibility and public support. The fundamental flaw would still remain, that the prospect of fines would be likely to discourage financial co-operation on the part of the publishers. The Committee at least was keen to remind the press that whatever regime was in place carried with it a high degree of responsibility, namely the burden of ensuring that the public had confidence in its delivery of news and media nationwide.

As we have seen, this stark lack of efficacy in keeping its house in order was exposed dramatically by the 2011 phone hacking scandal. This bombshell for the tabloid media, already Britain's most mischievous outlet for scandal, totally exposed and undermined the PCC. Even David Cameron was compelled to acknowledge that the phone hacking scandal had revealed the PCC to be *"ineffective and lacking in rigor"*[11], there being a need for *"a new system entirely"* that would be *"truly independent"*[12] of both the Government and the press on the basis that *"the press as regulated today is not working"*[13], and prompting an announcement from Baroness Buscombe that she would be stepping down as Chair of the PCC.[14]

In the wake of this scandal there has been a wide range of proposals for reform. The Director of the Media Standards Trust, Martin Moore has published what was aptly described as a spectrum of reforms in seven proposals as set out on his website[15]. In September 2011, Hugh Tomlinson QC, renowned expert in public and libel law, as well as a regular contributor to the legal section of the *Guardian*, analysed these reforms and produced an additional recommendation[16]. His arguments were based on the premise that the current system is based on mediation, whereas what is needed was regulation.

11 "Phone hacking scandal: Prime Minister says days of press self-regulation are over", *The Guardian*, 13 July 2011 (http://www.guardian.co.uk/media/2011/jul/13/pcc-phone-hacking)
12 Ibid
13 Ibid
14 "PCC confirms Baroness Buscombe is to step down", *The Guardian*, 29 July 2011 (http://www.guardian.co.uk/media/2011/jul/29/pcc-baroness-buscombe-to-step-down)
15 From Martin Moore's blog at Media Standards Trust: (http://mediastandardstrust.org/blog/reform-of-press-self-regulation-a-spectrum-of-possible-models/)
16 "Media Regulation – A Radical New Proposal" – Hugh Tomlinson QC on the *Inforrm* blog: (http://inforrm.wordpress.com/2011/09/29/media-regulation-a-radical-new-proposal-part-1-reform-options-hugh-tomlinson-qc/ (Part 1) And at: http://inforrm.wordpress.com/2011/09/30/media-regulation-a-radical-new-proposal-part-2-more-reform-options-hugh-tomlinson-qc/ (Part 2) And at: http://inforrm.wordpress.com/2011/10/04/media-regulation-a-radical-new-proposal-part-3-a-media-regulation-tribunal-hugh-tomlinson-qc/ (Part 3).)

The first of Martin Moore's proposals was to simply abolish the PCC and leave a vacuum of regulation, with no appointment of any watchdog, statutory or otherwise. If this were to be implemented it would create a position similar to that in the United States. Each publication would simply have to self-regulate to the extent it decided would be necessary to maintain the credibility of the content of its pages. This might, however, become extremely dependent on the readership for which the newspaper caters and their expectations – which is of course inexorably linked with revenue, and would be likely to result in a fairly benign "system", arguably even less satisfactory than the PCC.

If legal action was to become the only avenue for addressing complaints independently, this may create unfairness for those with more trivial complaints (as it is said, *de minimis non curat lex* – the law does not concern itself with trifles) or limited means, and ultimately result in more litigation. It would doubtless also leave a great sense of unease in terms of those expecting more positive measures to be implemented after the *News of the World* phone hacking scandal, leading to lack of public confidence in the press. This is a "ground-zero" option, the least severe or revolutionary part of the spectrum.

Moore's second suggestion would be to reform or augment the existing PCC, an option that is the preferred route of many within the industry. This is hardly surprising given that the PCC was originally the industry's own system of self-regulation. This would involve giving the organisation greater investigatory powers and, as had previously been implemented to create the impression of independence, increase the number of lay members. It was suggested that this new PCC could also possibly be given the ability to issue fines or impose other limited sanctions, as per the conclusions from the CMS report. The benefit of this would be that the framework is already in place and functioning to a level that, at least in terms of dealing with complaints and mediation, has been reported to be relatively effective. However, the basic problem with this proposal remains that adding further powers to the PCC would not address its fundamental constitutional flaws. As Moore reiterated, the modus operandi of the body is mediation, not regulation – Hugh Tomlinson QC was similarly of the opinion that the existing PCC would not handle the major culture shift that would be required for re-gearing of this nature. The effectiveness of the system would still be dependent on the extent to which the industry would be prepared to subscribe, and could easily be undone with further problems such as the *Northern and Shell* withdrawal.

In his third level, Moore suggests the establishment of a new independent body. This would still be exempted from strict legislative reforms, but would rather be a re-born version of the PCC that *would* be equipped to shoulder the burden of active monitoring and pro-active investigation. Similar to the *Advertising Standards Agency,* which regulates also subject to the voluntary subscription of its members, but also with Ofcom as it "arms-length regulatory backstop". This is cited as the most popular option – requiring little legislative work, but providing a new standard, independent from the industry's influence. The recourse available by way of a backstop would give this organisation some teeth and a tougher image. However, it appears that the fundamental flaws with a "floating", or voluntary, regulator could possibly be intensified. The press would still need to be incentivised to join – and this would be much more difficult given the likely opposition from the press and "freedom of speech" lobby to the statutory intervention. There could also be difficult questions as regards how the body would be funded, being a more expensive undertaking than the second option.

The fourth proposal was to broaden the remit of the established statutory broadcast regulator, Ofcom, to include the press so that it would transform into a regulator across all media. The difficulties with this would be in adapting the current Ofcom Code; rules such as the requirement for impartiality in broadcasting would have to be relaxed for the press. Ofcom is at least equipped to level fines and sanctions against those in breach of its code, although this regulator might not be considered to be as efficiently pro-active as would be expected at first glance.

Hugh Tomlinson coined the phrase "*Ofpress*" for this merger. However, this option would be likely to lead to more strident objections from the press and politicians – who are likely to claim that the statutory clout of Ofcom would place too much of a burden on the press and its freedom, or be regarded as a system of "government control." The press lobby is always quick to recite its constitutional entitlement to be able to criticize the government without fear of any penalty, or interference from the same government. While perhaps this would have to be broadly applied, the argument would probably be that this type of interface with a legislatively supported body would simply be too close for comfort. Another problem would be that this system, as well as the previous proposals, could not possibly address the difficulty in policing the third avenue of publication, the internet. There would always be an avenue available for those publishers who refuse to submit to regulation to simply re-locate their operation in the United States (or Iceland) and avoid any repercussions for publication of whatever they choose on the Internet (the web being labelled as the lawless "wild west" of the media).

The fifth option offered by Moore was the creation of a professional body for journalists, similar to the Law Societies in the UK and Ireland. Moore quotes John Lloyd from the Financial Times on this point:[17]

> "*A Journalism Society's stakeholders would include representatives of the government; the educational establishment; civil society (for instance relevant non-governmental organizations and policy institutes); industry and finance; and the news media. All of these would be committed, under its charter, to pluralist, independent, opinionated news media, working within the law.*"[18]

---

17 From Martin Moore's blog at Media Standards Trust: (http://mediastandardstrust.org/blog/reform-of-press-self-regulation-a-spectrum-of-possible-models/)

18 http://blogs.ft.com/the-a-list/2011/07/08/murdoch-broke-britains-press-this-is-how-we-fix-it/#axzz1ZLqrMi3j – restricted to Registered users. The exact quote reads:

> "*The Journalism Society's stakeholders should include representatives of the government; the educational establishment; civil society (for instance relevant non-government organisations and policy institutes); industry and finance; and the news media. All of these would be committed, under its charter, to pluralist, independent, opinionated news media, working within the law.*"

This form of professional registration would not impose any publication restrictions, but membership of the body could reflect a certification of quality and adherence to standards upheld by the new *Society*. The difficulties with this were pointed out quickly by Moore and Tomlinson. If the establishment of such an organisation were carried out under statute, as is the case for the Law Society, there would be complaints of the parallel with "licensing for journalists", which the press would doubtlessly argue would violate free speech principles. While the state may license lawyers and doctors, and in turn revoke such licenses on any misconduct, such actions being in the public interest, journalists would still be likely to find this hard to accept.

Moore's sixth proposal would be to, again, scrap the existing scheme of independent regulation, but in this instance carry out larger scale reforms in the *law* of media and privacy. The development of a more precise and wide ranging media law would accordingly motivate media organisations to devise their own systems of internal self-regulation, so as to minimise their potential liability.

The new law could be a codified consolidation of existing law incorporating additional proposals dealing with accuracy as well as ground-level matters such as a right to reply and the structure of complaints, retractions and apologies. Moore considered that this model would require a clear and strong public defence for journalists in order to protect their interests and right to freedom of expression. This should include consideration of factors such as the motivation behind the story as well the outcome, and the extent of harm. However, the principal difficulty would still remain that the Courts would become the key arbiter in dealing with media regulation issues. This would create the threat of *legalism*. If instances of publication were on a "knife edge" that could only be assessed by a team of lawyers, the pressure for expending greater resources in terms of legal fees both on the part of the publishers and the public or injured party would be greater.

The final and most progressive shade on the spectrum is the seventh proposal, suggesting a new statutory regulator for all media, with Tomlinson putting forward the title of the "Media Regulation Authority." This would stand in line with the lesser known publication of the second Calcutt report in 1993, which suggested the press had been given its chance to self-regulate effectively, but ultimately failed – and should be necessarily subject to a statutory regime. Using a model derived from Ofcom, a regulating body would be established to police conduct under a statutory framework, having been given powers such as being able to issue fines and restrict publication to sanction "offenders". Tomlinson suggested that there could further be a compensation scheme incorporated to provide for victims of false publication or invasion of privacy. Moore had aligned this option with the current systems for regulation of law, medicine and banking. The regulator should be able to offer a service to the public in addressing any of their complaints, as well as taking its own pro-active measures for maintaining standards – it could be extended to the digital domain as operated in this jurisdiction.

While this option would clearly be the most effective it would, as a result, also be the one that would meet with fierce opposition from politicians and the press, objecting to any type of "state regulation" or "government control" of the media.

A regime featuring the ability to impose fines and other sanctions would necessarily require use of the criminal law – and the association of publication in the media with crime would be considered extremely draconian and likely to induce the "chilling" effect, which is generally undesirable for a democratic society.

Hugh Tomlinson suggested a further "eighth option" in attempting to find a "half-way house" between the co-operative regulation and the introduction of a mandatory statutory regime. This was the proposition of the establishment of a Media Review Tribunal (MRT). In the first instance the MRT would be the adjudicator for a new "Media Code", to which publishers would be required to voluntarily submit. However, adherence to the code would provide the MRT member with protection from Court proceedings, as any complaints against it would be dealt by the MRT instead.

Mr Tomlinson raised a number of specific points in support of his vision for standards to be applied under the hypothetical MRT's Code, as follows:

● The focus of the Code could be on "factual inaccuracy" rather than "damage to reputation".

● In the case of less serious inaccuracies, the remedy could be confined to an order for the publication of a correction or apology, rather than an award of damages.

● In the case of factual inaccuracies the MRT could grant "declarations of falsity".

● In some categories of less serious case (or cases involving smaller publishers – bloggers or the regional press) there could be a compulsory "mediation" and complaints resolution system – which had to be used before formal claims were brought.

● The MRT could operate a "take down" procedure where online inaccuracies are alleged – with swift adjudications on take down requests in relation to online material.

● There could be a *New York Times v Sullivan* defence to claims relating to the publication of false information based on lack of malice – good faith publication in the public interest.

● Corporations which brought MRT claims could be limited to declaratory relief.

● There could be a clearly defined "privacy" regime, including public interest protections.

● There could be limits on damages and a special regime for legal costs – to promote access to justice whilst ensuring "equality of arms".[19]

He suggested that the Code would still have to be press friendly in order to strike enough of a balance against the threat of litigation to entice membership. It is notable

19 From Part 3 of Hugh Tomlinson QC's entry on the *Inforrm* blog: (http://inforrm.wordpress. com/2011/10/04/media-regulation-a-radical-new-proposal-part-3-a-media-regulation-tribunal-hugh-tomlinson-qc/)

and curious that protection of the *rights of the press* has become an indispensible consideration for anyone wishing to engage in this debate notwithstanding that it is the very *abuse* of those rights that led to a growing appreciation of the lack of effectiveness of press regulation.

Mr Charlie Potter BL of Blackstone Chambers, who is a former BBC producer, contemplated the scenario where more cynical publications would have little difficulty in making the choice to opt out of the Tomlinson scheme[20]. How would the costs of membership fees plus the more numerous claims and complaints likely to accrue via the MRT compare to the financial exposure in the case of the fewer actions pursued via the Courts – the costs of which for the claimant likely then to remain inhibitive? Potter did not just critique the MRT model but himself proposed the establishment of an independent regulator on a statutory footing similar in some respects to Martin Moore's fourth option, but with an emphasis on the principle of a "lighter touch" in terms of regulation, so as to avoid the emphasis on state imposition. Firstly he thought this body could refer to Ofcom's mandate in accordance with section 3(3) of the Communications Act 2003 – "*to have regard, in all cases to (a) the principles under which regulatory activities should be transparent, accountable, proportionate, consistent and targeted only at cases in which action is needed...*" He further pointed out that the regulator's code should be based on the standard of ethics inherent to responsible journalism as recognised in the case of *Mosley v UK*[21]. His view was that efforts to secure the adherence of any publication to a code and adjudication under a code could be prescribed to have "*particular regard to the important of the Convention right to freedom of expression*" as per section 12 of the Human Rights Act 1998. In short, to directly incorporate the values of the Convention into the new regulatory regime – this would doubtlessly assuage the press element that is arguing denial of Article 10 rights through regulation.

Indeed, the establishment of a Media Tribunal is already the subject of official debate in Australia[22]. In September 2011 the Australian Government established a high profile (led by former Justice of the Federal Court of Australia, Ray Finkelstein QC, with the assistance of Dr Matthew Ricketson, Professor of Journalism at Canberra University and a former practising journalist) independent inquiry into Media and Media Regulation. The inquiry's task is to examine the means for addressing complaints against the media and the effectiveness of the operating press code administered by the current self-regulator, the Australian Press Council. As well as looking at the relevance of the code in light of technological advances, more crucially, the inquiry will formally enquire into the prospect of a statutory media tribunal to be established to regulate.

20 "Self v State: The Search for a model of effective press regulation" – Charlie Potter, on the *Inforrm* blog: (http://inforrm.wordpress.com/2011/10/06/self-v-state-the-search-for-a-model-of-effective-press-regulation-charlie-potter/)
21 *Mosley v The United Kingdom* – 48009/08 [2011] ECHR 774 (10 May 2011)
22 "Super-regulator plan floated by media inquiry issues paper", 28 September 2011, http://www.theaustralian.com.au/media/super-regulator-plan-floated-by-media-inquiry-issues-paper/story-e6frg996-1226149147907

In an article for the *Inforrm* blog site[23], the former Legal Manager of *Times Newspapers*, Alastair Brett, did not pull any punches in suggesting that the PCC is *"in the operating theatre and in a critical condition"*[24], and commented that it was in need of *"a major blood transfusion and a complete set of canine implants*[25]*"*. Following on with his theme, he suggested that the PCC could be re-structured as the *"Office of Press Regulation and Adjudication"* (OPRA) with more streamline procedures[26]. Interestingly, Mr Brett suggested that the Body could be divided into two sections, with a "mediation" division offering services like the old PCC over breaches of its Code of Practice and "adjudication" division which would offer fast track adjudication of libel and privacy actions.

Although he was of the opinion that OPRA must be outside state control and be self-financing, which is likely to draw unfavourable comparisons with the current setup, he suggested that the adjudication would be similar to that used in the construction industry and be binding on the parties unless challenged in the Courts. However, while this is sound in theory, and indeed quite logical, the reality is that the press, as the primary financial contributors for whom OPRA will depend on for its very existence, may not be in a position to deal with the fundamental criticisms of self interest and protection, that would be avoided if Mr Brett's proposal were to be embodied in a statutory organisation with total and complete independence from the media.

A further interesting development arising from the Leveson Inquiry has been the approach taken by the *Daily Mail* Editor in Chief, Paul Dacre. Previously, any of Mr Dacre's public pronouncements had been considered to be staunchly anti-privacy[27]. However in the course of submissions to the PCC, Mr Dacre advocated his proposal *"to compel all newspaper owners to fund and participate in self-regulation"*[28]. His formula would have self-regulation being made a compulsory feature for large scale publication on a statutory basis, with the backstop being the appointment of a *Press Ombudsman* having the power *"to investigate, possibly with specialists co-opted onto his panel, potential press industry scandals. The Ombudsman could also have the power to summon journalists and editors to give evidence, to name offenders and, if necessary – in the cases of the most extreme malfeasance – to impose fines"*[29]. Perhaps this proposal could be described as being somewhat vague in terms of how it could in reality be implemented, and also strangely contradictory given that elsewhere in his speech Mr. Dacre had condemned the prospect of the PCC being able to impose fines. However the emergence of such a strong proposal from such a prominent figure in the media could perhaps reflect a sense of palpable tension within press ranks following on from the hacking scandal.

23   http://inforrm.wordpress.com/
24   "A sabre-toothed PCC for press complaints and libel actions?" – Alastair Brett', *Inforrm* (http://inforrm.wordpress.com/2011/10/09/a-sabre-toothed-pcc-for-press-complaints-and-libel-actions-alastair-brett/)
25   Ibid
26   Ibid
27   http://inforrm.wordpress.com/2011/10/16/the-story-most-papers-missed-dacre-calls-for-statutory-backstop-martin-moore/
28   http://hackinginquiry.org/news/paul-dacres-talk-at-leveson-inquiry-seminar/
29   Ibid

Chapter 12 Who guards the guardians?

From a review of the aforesaid proposals, it appears that the debate surrounding reform will be extensive and controversial. Many of the above proposals appear unworkable in the climate that has developed, where the press will still clamour for as close to unlimited freedom to publish as they can possibly achieve in the circumstances. Perhaps it will ultimately be the public, influenced by Lord Justice Leveson's findings, who will decide how far the press will be allowed to go in terms of intrusive and improper investigations. Bearing in mind that with the commercial considerations involved it is the readership which will always have the ultimate sanction in deciding whether to buy a newspaper that is seen to have abused its position to the detriment of the common good.

Chapter 13

Conclusion

> *"Law never is, but is always about to be"*
>
> (Benjamin Cardozo)

So what was it that created the dynamics for this so called clash with press freedom? Was it really a genuine disquiet with our libel laws, bearing in mind that the laws, notwithstanding the introduction of the Defamation Act in 1996 in the UK, have retained the same basic principles for the past couple of centuries. The media frenzy regarding the so called "chilling effect" of the law is very much a recent phenomenon, which has gained and maintained momentum despite the fact that the number of defamation Actions in general has been falling significantly during the past decade, and fewer and fewer cases are reaching trial. Indeed, the instances of so called *libel tourism* are even less in number and, in the overall scale of things, would not have posed a genuine threat to the financial coffers of the media corporations.

While on one view the press cannot be blamed for striking out in their own defence, it is a shame that they have not chosen to adopt anything approaching an open-minded and balanced approach. For example, by affording column inches to both sides of the argument, and highlighting, in particular, the almost impossible financial hurdles facing the "man on the street", in circumstances where he may have been genuinely libelled with a devastating impact on his personal and professional reputation.

The reality appears to be that the momentum for what surely has been the most successful campaign since that undertaken on behalf of the tobacco industry several decades ago had been triggered by the stance taken by Dr Rachel Ehrenfeld. The impact of her initial protestations had been to allow the powerful publishers' associations in the US to vent their frustration, which has been done with alarming speed and effectiveness, with the willing support of typically fawning politicians.

As has been outlined in the chapters of this book, the joint efficiency of the press and the politicians has been clearly illustrated by the rapid progress of the legislation at an unprecedented rate, particularly in America, even with the distraction of the world's economic woes entering every aspect of public and private life.

Having observed such astounding success in the United States under the auspices of a First Amendment campaign, the British press could hardly believe their luck and had no hesitation in taking the lead from their American counterparts in adopting a similarly intense and unsubtle strategy.

Such was the "brotherhood" and common cause as between media empires on both sides of the Atlantic that basic principles of international comity were ignored or trampled over in wanton disregard for the respect for another country's legal culture.

Indeed, it would be very interesting to see the reaction of the US lawmakers if similar legislation were passed by Parliament prohibiting the enforcement of US judgments against British companies that were deemed to offend UK legal principles. One example would be the extraordinary, and many would say grossly excessive, fees charged by US attorneys, which often equate to a deduction of more than 50% of the damages awarded. Often these fees can run to hundreds of millions of dollars and have led to the universal disparagement of lawyers in the United States. Nonetheless, the Courts in that country still permit such deductions from an injured person's award of damages. This would generally be regarded as totally unacceptable under UK and Irish law, and indeed provides a stark contrast to the parallel press campaign demanding a reduction in the contingency legal fees awarded to Claimant solicitors in libel Actions.

Another instance of double standards was highlighted in the US Government's attitude towards Julian Assange, the Wikileaks founder who had gained access to, and disseminated internationally, extremely sensitive US Government information. The outcry against Assange and the efforts to discredit and bring him down were swift and ruthless, albeit not particularly effective in no small measure due to the US legislators' inability to interfere with freedom of speech or breaches of privacy to a level similar to that prevailing in other parts of the world. As to whether the Wikileaks fiasco leads to a reassessment of these American values remains to be seen.

In considering the UK Government's draft Defamation Bill, Lord Mawhinney succinctly outlined four core principles to be addressed by the House of Commons Joint Committee, namely:

(i)   Freedom of Expression/Protection of Reputation: Some aspects of current law and procedure should provide greater protection to freedom of expression. This is a key foundation of any society. Reputation is established over years and the law needs to provide due protection against unwarranted serious damage;

(ii) Reducing Costs: The reduction in the extremely high costs of defamation proceedings is essential to limiting the chilling effect and making access to legal redress a possibility for the ordinary citizen. Early resolution of disputes is not only key to achieving this, but is desirable in its own right – in ensuring that unlawful injury to reputation is remedied as soon as possible and that claims do not succeed or fail merely on account of the prohibitive cost of legal action. Courts should be the last rather than the first resort;

(iii) Accessibility: Defamation law must be made easier for the ordinary citizen to understand and afford, whether they are defending their reputation or their right to free speech; and

(iv) Cultural change: Defamation law must adapt to modern communication culture, which can be instant, global, anonymous, very damaging and potentially outside the reach of the Courts[1].

These principles would appear to effectively summarise the fundamental issues at stake, but it remains to be seen whether any statutory intervention can improve the safe-guarding of freedom of speech on the one hand, while at the same time protecting the rights of the individual together with scientific and academic debate. As Lord Mawhinney pointed out in summarising the Committee's objectives:

"The practical realities of policing a global conversation, straddling different legal jurisdictions, require us to adopt imaginative means of mitigating the serious damage to reputation that can be wrought at the click of a button".[2]

The fundamental problem of enforcement against internet service providers based outside the jurisdiction and reach of the European Courts will not be resolved by even the most robust legislation, as has been borne out by the difficulties in litigating against a vindictive online publisher as matters currently stand.

Likewise, while the basic substance of the draft Defamation Bill appears on the surface to be reasonable, and in some ways understandable, the practicalities involved in enforcement and securing access to justice for members of the public are essentially left hanging in the air.

Much has been made by the government and indeed Lord Lester on whose draft Bill much of the proposed changes have been based, of the need to improve clarity of the law and protect freedom of speech, academic debate and responsible journalism. As to whether the clarification offered in relation to the defences of "substantial truth" and "honest opinion" will not simply lead to more extensive legal arguments in the Courts remains to be seen. Certainly the press will be very satisfied with the proposal to abandon the right to trial by jury in all but the most exceptional cases. The more robust approach advocated towards libel tourism will also be music to many an editor's ears. However, the reality may turn out to be that the most effective change in the law will be the "single publication rule". The introduction of this rule would protect any re-publication of the same material in a similar manner after it has been in the public domain for a period of more than one year, although further clarification will be required regarding the various scenarios arising from the transfer of a paper-based publication on to the internet.

Perhaps one of the most promising proposals arising from the Joint Committee's recommendations is the move towards mediation and arbitration. Although forms of alternative dispute resolution of this nature have generally received a lukewarm approach from the press in the past, effective judicial intervention and encouragement could be the key in creating momentum to what must surely be an obvious and expedient alternative to costly and lengthy litigation. Such an approach

1   Joint Committee on the Draft Defamation Bill, *First Report* (2011) para 16
     http://www.publications.parliament.uk/pa/jt201012/jtselect/jtdefam/203/20302.htm
2   Ibid page 4

would be in tandem with the general groundswell of support for mediation in relation to other types of commercial disputes and litigation. However, voluntary mediation may only achieve acceptability and momentum if the Government are prepared to introduce similar "mediate before you litigate" legislation similar to the Californian model, rather than simply allow the parties to adopt a selective approach on a case by case basis.

In the meantime, in the UK the outcry for a relaxation in our defamation laws continues unabated, notwithstanding the phone hacking and other related scandals that would clearly suggest the need for a strengthening, if not of our defamation laws, then of the protection of our fundamental right to privacy. If we are to achieve genuine freedom of speech and expression in the media there must be fairness and even-handedness across the board. All sides are agreed that access to justice, particularly in the Courts, should not be limited to the wealthier sections of our society and that investigative journalism is only worthwhile if it is based on sound facts and objectives to expose a wrong, rather than to sensationalise a story for commercial reasons.

Investigative journalists perform a vital service to society and are entitled to and must be given, appropriate and proportionate protection. They should be free from financial and other pressures from both external and internal sources. In order to achieve this balance and to distinguish this good work from the gossip and titillation of the tabloids, careful and focused changes in the law ought to be carefully considered and introduced. The problem is that the laws of libel, just like any other law, cannot be all things to all men, and therefore responsibility rests with the legislators and those politicians who have a genuine desire to protect their electorate, to ensure fair treatment for both press and public alike. This will be no mean feat and unfortunately the most recent debates on statutory reform in the UK appear to suggest merely reactive tweaks to the previous legislation, which do not specifically address the rights of the citizen and the genuine investigative journalist who, in my respectful submission, form the two groups that are entitled to most consideration.

Finally, while we can all debate the fairness or otherwise of our privacy and defamation laws and the conflicting attitudes towards the fundamental underlying principles, the bottom line is that unless there is an adequate deterrent, particularly in the case of privacy and confidentiality, then the law, however apparently unfair to one side or the other, is totally undermined. Unfortunately, the undermining of the right to privacy, confidentiality and reputation have one thing in common – once breached the damage is done and can never really be properly or adequately remedied, never mind reinstated.

Freedom of speech should and must be for everyone and not just limited to specific individuals or causes selected by the press at any given time. The public want and is entitled to hear both sides of the story, and be allowed to make up their own minds as to the merits of any particular argument or issue. And equally of course the press, if this basic right is acknowledged, should be allowed to report freely and transparently on the controversial matters of the day. It would be sad indeed if the broadsheets in particular, were consigned to the historical archives because their reputation as a bastion of truth and credibility had been gradually eroded, allowing the internet news providers to take their place.

Index

Index